D1236568

DEPRESSION

NEAL H. OLSHAN, Ph.D.

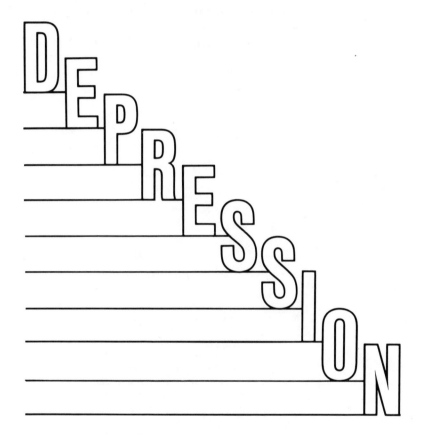

FRANKLIN WATTS
NEW YORK|LONDON|TORONTO|SYDNEY|1982

ACKNOWLEDGMENTS

Mary Lou Sargent for manuscript preparation
and technical suggestions.

Jerry Bockmon, Harriet Wise, Annelise Loeser,
and Carol Dagg for accurate readings.

Mary, Sandy, Bobby, and Maureen, who provided
the support and understanding that made
the work possible.

Library of Congress Cataloging in Publication Data

Olshan, Neal.
Depression.

Bibliography: p.
Includes index.
Summary: Discusses causes of and treatments for
depressive illness, a mental disorder characterized
by changes in sleep patterns and loss of interest
in food and normal day-to-day activities.
1. Depression, Mental—Juvenile literature.
[1. Depression, Mental. 2. Mental illness] I. Title.
RC537.047 1982   616.85'27·   82-11004
ISBN 0-531-04496-3

5

CONTENTS

DEPRESSION

PREFACE

Depressive illness may occur among people of all ages, socioeconomic classes, races, and cultures. It is the most prevalent form of mental illness but also by far the most responsive to treatment.

Many people suffer needlessly, unaware that their "blue" feelings, poor appetite, problems with sleeping, and feelings of exhaustion may all be symptoms of a serious underlying depression. Some people don't go for help even if the symptoms persist because they expect they will eventually recover on their own, as they have in the past.

But severe depression, or even the more common mild depression, should not be confused with ordinary feelings of unhappiness that everyone experiences—the times of sadness associated with unhappy events or failures, or the emotional letdowns that may occur around holidays such as Christmas. Nor should severe depression be confused with grief brought about by the loss (death, divorce) of a loved one.

Sadness or grief—for a limited period of time—are normal reactions to life's stresses, failures, and disappointments. In contrast, the person afflicted with a depressive disorder, often referred to as *clinical depression*, remains severely depressed for an unusually long period, thus indicating that the depression might not have been caused by the incident alone. A person with a depressive disorder has trouble functioning in normal day-to-day activities. In fact, some psychiatrists and psychologists think that the major symptom of clinical depression is drastic change— a former good student loses interest in school; a typically active person can't get out of bed in the morning; or an individual who normally enjoys his or her work loses interest in the job. The loss of interest in food and changes in sleep patterns or other symptoms commonly experienced by depressed people may continue for months, even years, if not treated properly.

In recent years significant gains have been made in understanding and treating depression. This book describes depressive disorders, possible causes, therapies used in treating depression, and ways in which you, as a friend or family member, can help a depressed person.

CHAPTER ONE

DEPRESSION: AN OVERVIEW

_____

_____

_____

_____

_____

_____

_____

_____

_____

_____

_____

_____

Hippocrates, who lived in the fourth century B.C., gave the first medical description of depression, which he called "melancholia," believing it to be caused by an excess of black bile in the brain. He concluded that melancholia was closely related to epilepsy, and he categorized it with mania, phrenitis, and paranoia as one of the four major types of psychiatric illness.

Although Hippocrates might have been the first to describe the disorder, it was Aretaeus of Cappadocia who, in the second century A.D., wrote the most complete and remarkably modern depiction of depression. Aretaeus proposed that depression was caused by purely psychological factors, and that it had little to do with bile, phlegm, or other "humors" (body fluids). He was also the first to associate mania—excessive elation or hyperactivity—with depression, considering both conditions as part of a single disease entity and accurately noting that the illness recurred despite remissions and that recovery from one episode did not ensure a cure. Finally, Aretaeus appreciated the significance of interpersonal relationships in the course of depression, reporting the case of a severely disturbed patient who recovered when he fell in love.

With the fall of Rome to the barbarian hordes, most of the progress made during the Greco-Roman era was lost. It was a dark time in human history; mental illness was generally attributed to possession by demons, with exorcism as the principal form of treatment. The rites of exorcism typically included prayers, incantations, visits to shrines, noise-making, and forced feeding of the possessed person with concoctions of such things as sheep dung and wine.

Abnormal behavior in the Middle Ages was often characterized by episodes of mass madness such as flagellantism (self-injury), tarantism (dancing mania), and lycanthropy (the delusion that one is an animal). Epidemics of this kind continued through the fifteenth and sixteenth centuries and even, though somewhat abated, into the seventeenth century.

The bizarre behavior exhibited by the mentally ill was at that time considered part of the "will of God." Yet, psychotic or depressed individuals often became the victims of religious persecutions. People who worked to expose others who had "sold their souls to the devil" were certain they would receive salvation for their efforts.

Witchcraft mania, which flourished in Europe around this time, did not erupt in the American colonies until the late seventeenth century. Many suspected of being witches were hunted down, tortured, maimed, and killed; and the Inquisition in Europe marked a low point in the victimization of emotionally disturbed persons. By the time of the last known execution of a "witch," in Switzerland in 1782, the belief that aberrant behavior was due to psychological causes was gathering momentum.

In fact, as far back as the sixteenth century, the beliefs and practices surrounding demonology and witchcraft were already being challenged. Johann Weyer (1515–1588), a physician who wrote under the Latin name of Johannes Weirus, studied witchcraft and published a book on the subject. In his book, Weyer suggested that many individuals who had been imprisoned, tortured, or burned for witchcraft were really just mentally ill. Weyer's conclusion evoked strong protests from theologians and physicians of his day.

Enlightened individuals such as Weyer had been concerned about the mentally ill for several hundred years, but the revolution in thought that culminated in modern psychiatry and psychology really began with the work of Philippe Pinel (1745–1826). As chief physician at LeBicetre Hospital in Paris, Pinel began the then-unheard-of practices of talking with his patients, keeping records, and assembling case histories. He achieved great success with his experiments in treating the mentally ill with kindness and consideration. Patients were unchained, were moved out of dungeons into clean, cheerful rooms, and were permitted to walk around the hospital grounds. Pinel's pupil Esquirol (1772–1840) added other innovations and set up a new system of mental hospitals in France. In addition, by tabulating what he considered to be the probable psychological causes of various disorders, he made the first attempt to apply crude statistical methods to diagnosing emotional disorders. However, most of the psychological causes described by Esquirol, such as a sudden financial loss or disappointment in love, were objective events in the life of the patient. This made his results often questionable and very incomplete.

At the same time that asylums were being reformed in France, the English Quaker, William Tuke, established York Retreat, a private estate where mental patients could live in a warm, spiritual atmosphere free of the punitiveness of most asylums. However, since these initial advances in the humane treatment of mental patients were vigorously resisted by the general populace, additional such facilities did not become available until the end of the nineteenth century.

More modern concepts of the causes of clinical depression emerged when theorists finally abandoned their reliance on purely physical explanations of emotional disorders. By the beginning of the twentieth century, a broader view of human behavior was evolving, in which social and cultural influences were accorded a major role in the formation of the depressive state.

Modern psychiatry owes much of its real foundation to the work of the Viennese physician Sigmund Freud (1856–1939). Freud went to France in 1885 to study under French physicians in Paris. During this time Freud, who was intrigued by the mysteries of hysteria and depression, began to formulate a theory involving the effects of unconscious experiences on conscious and overt behavior.

In Vienna, Freud used hypnosis with his patients but abandoned this method when he found that hysterical or depressed patients returning for further therapy displayed new symptoms in place of the ones that had been removed through hypnosis—a phenomenon he called symptom substitution. For hypnosis he substituted the technique of free association, in which the patient simply talked about whatever came to mind. He believed that this seemingly random conversation would ultimately reveal the basis of the patient's problems. From Freud's method of free association and his interpretations of patients' dreams and behavior came modern psychoanalysis. One of Freud's most famous pupils, Carl Gustav Jung (1875–1961), was instrumental in developing psychoanalytical treatment of psychosis and depression.

Freud's contemporary, Emil Kraepelin (1856–1926), a German pioneer in psychiatry, was extremely dissatisfied with his day's system of diagnosing psychiatric disorders and began researching common symptoms of various mental disorders in an attempt to classify those disorders and simplify diagnosis. Kraepelin wrote a textbook on psychiatry that was revised many times after its first edition in 1883.

Wilhelm Reich's studies of character analysis constituted a valuable contribution to the body of psychoanalytic theory. Karl Abraham emphasized the importance of infant development for later psychological functioning. In 1911, Dr. Abraham published his first in a series of papers specifically on depression.

Since the time of Freud, Kraepelin, and Abraham, researchers have continued to explore the best ways to diagnose and treat depression. Scientists are working worldwide to explore the newest theories of chemical or genetic causes of depression.

The need for better diagnostic methods for all types of mental disorders has led to publication of the *Diagnostic and Statistical Manual* (Third Edition) by the American Psychiatric Association. Sections of this work devoted specifically to depression provide psychiatrists, psychologists, and physicians with the most up-to-date information to be used for the proper diagnosis of depressive illness.

WHAT IS DEPRESSION?

We use the term *depression* in everyday life to refer to the feeling usually described as "the blues" or "being down." This feeling may occur in rainy weather, during an annoying cold, or after an argument with a friend. Sometimes an event that is usually expected to be happy ends with "blue" feelings. People commonly experience "the blues" on holidays such as Christmas or New Year's Day, after moving into a new house, starting at a new school, celebrating a birthday, entering a new classroom, or—for women—following childbirth. A clinical depression, as opposed to a "normal" depression, refers to a prolongation or exaggeration of these normal reactions to stress and disappointment, may or may not follow a stressful event, and is probably not caused by the stressful event alone.

Scientists have investigated and performed experiments based on the idea that "normal" people who are around depressed people for any length of time may actually become depressed themselves. The results of the experiments suggest that depressive behavior causes other people to avoid the depressed individual and that people usually prefer nondepressed individuals as friends.

Many times the depressed person will tend to compare himself or herself with nondepressed people, which may further increase and deepen the depression. Every encounter with a nondepressed person can become an opportunity for more depression.

Depression was the first disorder described by Freud in which he said the central cause was emotion rather than the sexual wish. To Freud melancholia was grief gone haywire—excessive, drawn out, often unrelated to anything happening in the environment, and seemingly unjustified.

One form of depression that has received a great deal of attention over the years is manic-depressive illness, in which a person is subject to severe mood swings, shifting quite suddenly from a deeply depressed to a manic state. The manic episode may last from a few hours to many weeks. In the manic state the person may become careless, flamboyant in appearance and extremely animated, may speak more rapidly than usual, and will have great difficulty concentrating.

As we can see, then, the term *depression* has many different meanings. It may be thought of as a mood, an emotion, or an illness. There are few people who, at one time or another, have not felt depressed, or "down."

Increasingly, we are finding that very young children, adolescents, and the elderly are as susceptible to depressive illness as anyone else. We now know that all human beings, regardless of sex, age, race, culture, religion, education, or economic status can experience depression or have serious depressive disorders.

SOCIOCULTURAL FACTORS IN DEPRESSION

The incidence of affective disorders in various societies and cultures has always interested scientists. Are the causes of depression global? In other words, do people experience depression in the same manner no matter where they live?

In early studies, J. C. Carothers found manic disorders fairly common among the East Africans he studied but pure depressive disorders relatively rare—the exact opposite of their incidence in the United States. He attributed the low incidence of depressive disorders in Africa to the fact that in traditional African cultures the individual is not usually held personally responsible for failures and misfortunes.

Dr. Carothers conducted his initial research in 1947. Needless to say, much has changed in Africa since these observations were made, and, in fact, more recent data suggest quite a different picture. In general, it appears that as societies become more "advanced," like those of Western Europe and the United States, their members become more prone to the development of what might be called Western-style depressive disorders.

Even in nonindustrialized countries where depressive disorders are relatively common, they seem less closely associated with feelings of guilt and self-recrimination than in the developed countries. In fact, among several groups of Australian aborigines, researchers have found not only an absence of guilt and self-recrimination in depressive reactions but also almost no incidence of attempted suicide. In some of these non-Western cultures the symptoms of depression are not even recognized as part of a depressive state. There may not even be in the society a concept of depression that would reasonably compare to our own.

In our own society, the role of sociocultural factors in depression remains unclear, but it would appear that the kinds of stress we experience in particular lead to a higher incidence of these as well as other disorders. High rates of divorce, constant striving for self-betterment, plus stresses in school and in growing up all appear, within our society, to increase the chances for depression—and may also be some of the results of depression.

Based on all the research conducted cross-culturally in the area of depression, it appears that no culture is free from incidence of depression, but each culture may express that depression in a different manner. Depression in its numerous forms is truly a worldwide problem.

DEPRESSION IS NOT NEW

Problems with depression are not new in the history of humankind. Descriptions of depressive disorders are found in the early writings of the Egyptians, Greeks, Hebrews, and Chinese. Many allusions to depression are found in the literary works of Shakespeare, Dostoevsky, Poe, and Hemingway. Saul, king of Israel in the eleventh century B.C., suffered from manic-depressive episodes, and King George III of England was subject to periods of manic overactivity, although it is now believed that George's maniacal behavior was a symptom of a serious physical disease known as porphyria. The list of historical figures who suffered from recurrent depression is a long one and includes such celebrated figures as Moses, Rousseau, Queen Victoria, Lincoln, Tchaikovsky, and Freud (the father of modern psychiatry). It appears that depression is a mental disorder common to the whole human race, both cross-culturally and historically.

INCIDENCE OF DEPRESSION

Depression is an epidemic that University of Pennsylvania's Martin Seligman estimates costs Americans up to $4 billion a year in lost work and medical bills. At the 1981 meeting of the American Psychiatric Association, depression was called the "common cold" of mental illness. Its social cost is enormous—broken marriages, troubled children, suicide, and even homicide. The National Institute of Mental Health says that one in every five Americans—about forty million people—will experience a clinical depression at some point during their lives. At any one time about 2.4 million people suffer from severe depression.

"Depression is a national disaster. It breaks up marriages, costs jobs, hampers the capacity to mother," says Maggie Scarf, author of *Unfinished Business: A Study of Depression in Women.* "Depression occurs more often in women than men, according to the studies, and women attempt suicide twice as often as men, usually with drugs and alcohol," she continues. Some researchers hypothesize that women are more willing than men to admit to depression and to seek help. If so, the statistics referring to the numbers of depressed men may be deceptively low.

The emotional pain of depression can be fatal. One in two hundred episodes of severe depression ends in suicide. For each suicide, ten depression victims try to kill themselves. Men more often complete the suicide attempt because the methods they employ are more lethal and the physical damage caused is less easily reversed.

RECOGNITION OF DEPRESSION

Clinical depression has probably always existed, but it was not recognized by most people as a true medical disorder until as recently as thirty years ago. Although doctors estimate that depression is the real cause for seeking medical help in approximately 30 percent of the patients they see, mild depression, which would benefit greatly from professional treatment, is usually not recognized as such.

Two prominent features of depression are almost always present: a dysphoric mood (sad, blue, hopeless, irritable, or worried) and a loss of interest or pleasure in almost all usual activities and pastimes. Someone who is depressed may be observed to have one or a combination of the following signs or symptoms:

Change of appetite
Weight change
   (usually a loss, but sometimes a gain)
Alteration in sleep patterns
   (insomnia or hypersomnia)
Loss of energy
Psychomotor changes
   (either agitation or increased slowness of response)
Feelings of self-reproach
Guilt
Difficulty thinking or concentrating
Frequent thoughts of death or suicide

WHO GETS DEPRESSED
AND WHY

Frustration, disappointment, or a personal loss of any kind will make almost anyone feel down. Each of us is different in our ability to deal with stressful situations, and some of us seem more vulnerable than others to developing the exaggerated response to stress called depression. In addition, depression can occur without unusual stress and can happen at any time from the cradle to the grave.

Numerous public figures have experienced depression. Winston Churchill, who referred to his attacks as "the black dog," once remarked that when this mood struck him he sometimes wondered whether he should just hurl himself in front of a train and end it all. Biographers have often referred to Abraham Lincoln's "melancholy face" and the "cadence of deep sadness in his voice." Twenty-five years before he was elected president, after breaking his engagement to Ann Rutledge, Lincoln fell into a severe depression that was at the time called "hypochondrism." Novelists F. Scott Fitzgerald and Fëdor Dostoevsky were known to be chronically downhearted. Vincent Van Gogh's low spirits became a major influence on his painting.

Virginia Woolf was a shy, creative English novelist who suffered from increasingly severe bouts of depression throughout her life. Some of her depression has been traced to the strong negative feelings she had toward her stern Victorian father, with her depression increasing significantly after his death. Friends also noticed an increase in her depression when her mother had died nine years earlier. In 1941, while in a state of deep depression, she wrote a suicide note to her husband, then jumped into the River Ouse and drowned.

DEPRESSION IN CHILDREN

Many people think of childhood as a happy time of little responsibility, much play, and endless enjoyment. Why is it, then, that so many children have thoughts such as, "I'm dumb, ugly, and stupid," "I wish I were dead," and "Nobody loves me." Why do so many children appear sad and blue?

Why do they describe themselves as never doing anything right? Why do they sometimes cry for what seems no reason at all?

Feeling down or sad are typical signs of depression in children. So are a lack of smiling and laughing, being unable to enjoy pets, and being unable to enjoy playing with other children, particularly happy children. It has been estimated that, like adults, 20 percent of children will suffer from depression at one time or another. Children show other signs of depression, too. They may feel

Agitated
Tired all the time
Seclusive (want to stay away from others)
Helpless
Hopeless
Worthless
Unloved
Used

Their schoolwork may suffer, and just going to school may require a terrible effort. Children may also have problems sleeping, lose their appetite, and complain of aches and pains without any apparent physical cause. Some severely depressed children even make suicidal threats, and a few even carry them out. These symptoms seem to be most common in children eight to eleven years old but may also appear in children older than eleven.

A sense of worthlessness or guilt and an attitude of self-deprecation appear in most cases of childhood depression. Some child psychiatrists believe that a certain percentage of "hyperactive" children may actually be suffering from depressive illness.

Symptoms of depression in children were recognized by medical writers as far back as the seventeenth century.

In the mid-nineteenth century, suicide and melancholia (blue feelings) were noted in children. But it was not until the early twentieth century that doctors reported symptoms of what we now know as severe depression in children. By the mid-1940s, doctors stated that children under one year of age that were separated from their mothers could experience depression. Investigators at the National Institute of Mental Health found that many young depressed patients had experienced long-term rejection by parents or loved ones. However, a direct connection between parental loss or rejection and childhood depression has never been clearly demonstrated.

When family life is poor, such as when there is excessive arguing between parents, constant fighting between brothers and sisters, or divorce, then young children may become depressed. In such situations children feel rejected and unloved. Other upsetting occurrences, such as failure in school, being punished, moving to a new neighborhood, or losing friends, could also lead to depression (though in some cases failure in school or losing friends could be a *result* of depression instead of a cause). But rarely does a young child become as deeply depressed as an adult; youngsters seem to be, in some ways, emotionally more resilient.

Depressed children often complain of stomachaches or headaches or misbehave in school. They may feel insecure, not want to eat (lack of appetite), eat all the time, be restless, or generally feel bad all over.

Even babies can become depressed. This is particularly true when a loving mother is absent or when they feel emotional neglect or sense the mother herself is depressed. Dr. Joseph Teicher, director of the Division of Child Psychiatry at the University of Southern California School of Medicine, observes: "Clinically, such infants show feeding disorders such as repeated regurgitation [throwing-up], slowness of movement, poor muscle tone, and excessive sleeping...these infants look like depressed little old men and women."

DEPRESSION IN TEENAGERS

Rebellion, doing poorly in school, constant arguing, running away, threats, dysphoria—all may be signs of teenage depression, though it is considered "normal" for teenagers to experience frequent low moods, which are related to the problems and pressures of becoming an adult.

Most often a teenager's depression will disappear in a short time. But if the teenager has a long history of difficulties and continuing problems, this may be evidence of an underlying depression. When rebellion, withdrawal, running away, and other attempts to reverse the depression fail to bring relief, the teenager may see suicide as the only solution to the problems of life. In reality, the attempted suicide is often a desperate cry for help. Sometimes the cry is not heard, and the attempt results in death. Suicide is the third leading cause of death among teenagers.

YOUNG ADULTS

Among college students and young adults, failure in the face of constant and intense competition often leads to or precedes depression or may even be a result of depression. Some students drop out of college because of depression. Highly ambitious men and women may set career goals that seem far out of reach, leading to episodes of depression.

Work at this time, too, may become disappointing or boring. Loss of employment or the need to move a family because of unemployment may cause people to feel suddenly worthless and dejected.

TABLE 1
PRECIPITATING CIRCUMSTANCES
IN 31 SUICIDES
OF CHILDREN AGES 12 TO 14

	Boy	Girl	Total
Disciplinary crisis	8	3	11 (36%)
Fight with peer other than close friend of opposite sex	3	1	4 (13.33%)
Dispute with close friend of opposite sex	1	2	3 (10%)
Dispute with parent	1	2	3 (10%)
Being dropped from a school team	2	0	2 (7%)
Fantasy "model"	1	1	2 (7%)
Interaction with psychotic parent	2	0	2 (9%)
No precipitant disclosed	3	0	3 (10%)

Shaffer, 1974, p. 279

MIDDLE AGE

In her mid-thirties to mid-forties, a nonworking married woman may feel trapped by the humdrum routine at home, seeing herself as "just a housewife." She may want to return to school or get a job; if she feels ineffectual or unable to change her situation, depression can set in. A man, facing the realization of middle age, may feel a failure in his job and, submerged in family pressures, may easily fall into depression.

The number of individuals who are depressed may start to increase during middle age. Affected by the familiar "middle-age syndrome," people see their youth fading, their physical reserves more easily depleted. Men lose their hair and gain weight and see themselves as aging quickly. Their self-image begins to sink. It is not unusual for a depressed forty-year-old man to talk about feeling useless and about his life being "finished."

But middle-aged men are not the only ones so affected. In fact, some researchers maintain that depression occurs in middle-aged women two to three times as often as in men. The reasons vary, ranging from hormonal disturbances to repressed rebellion against "male-dominated society" and insecurity about their roles as women, wives, and mothers. In middle age, women may become despondent at the sight of wrinkles and expanding waistlines, and they often worry about losing their attractiveness to men. Both men and women may find their marriages, jobs, and family life taking a back seat to depression.

Menopause may trigger a difficult period for women, to whom losing the ability to have children becomes a traumatic event. Anxiety and chronic stress combined with a sense of unfulfillment can give depression a chance to take root.

For women especially, but also for many men, middle age can be a time of loneliness and aimlessness, when children are grown and leave home. As retirement nears, with yet another change in life, people again seem to become highly susceptible to depression.

THE ELDERLY

The elderly may be the most vulnerable to depression, but, unfortunately, their depression is often regarded as a result of old-age senility (inability to think clearly). They are the most likely people in our society to have suffered loss of friends and family, financial resources, familiar places, health, and a feeling of belonging and usefulness.

Loss of physical strength and flexibility, adjusting to being dependent on other people, financial insecurity, plus a sense of not being needed—these are some of the reasons why so many elderly people become depressed.

Biological changes are taking place in the various systems within the body. Physically there is a loss of good eyesight, hearing, teeth, and hair. Depressive reactions to such changes are a major problem for the elderly.

The elderly are likely to develop a deep and enduring depression over the death of a relative or longtime friend. In their age group, they continue to see people around them dying. And, understandably, they may be despondent about the inevitability and, at times, seeming closeness of their own death. Often, the elderly person's depression is camouflaged by constant complaints of physical problems or aches and pains for which there is no physical finding. In these cases the symptoms may be psychosomatic.

Depression among older persons worsens if it is not recognized and properly treated. It can end in suicide. In fact, the highest recorded rate of suicide is in men over age sixty.

Diagnosing depression in the elderly can be a very difficult and at times frustrating task for the physician. Memory loss, confused thinking, or apathy symptomatic of senility may actually be caused by depression. On the other hand, awakening early in the morning and reduced appetite, typical of depression in younger people, are common among older persons who are not depressed. Additionally, certain medications taken by the elderly or poor diets may lead to depression as a side effect. As mentioned earlier, the older person will often not admit to feelings of depression but instead may blame the depressive symptoms on physical ailments.

Treatment of elderly depressed persons may be complicated by physical problems. Before prescribing any antidepressant drug for an elderly person, a physician must carefully evaluate all other drugs used by the patient, to avoid unpleasant or dangerous side effects. Even with all the difficulties involved in diagnosis and treatment of depression in elderly people, however, there is no reason, with the advances in modern science, that anyone of this age group should remain undiagnosed and untreated.

In sum, while the reasons for depression in each age group may differ, depression is not unique to any one age group. And the underlying causes of depression for all age groups seem to be the stresses of disappointment and loss.

DEPRESSION AS
AN ATTEMPT
TO COMMUNICATE

Therapists frequently consider depressive behavior to be an attempt to communicate a specific message to, or to get the attention of, a loved one—specifically a friend, parent, or spouse. Many times such behavior is equivalent to saying, "I want you to notice me and understand how I'm feeling." Unfortunately, this communication may not be understood, and the depression could actually become worse. The depressed person may then feel that no one understands him or her, cares, or is willing to help. In other words, using depression as a method of communication may be a vicious circle that only leads to further and deeper depression.

DEPRESSION CAN MAKE YOU SICK

Is it possible that depression can make people sick? The answer appears to be yes. There is increasing evidence that chronic depression may be involved in a host of illnesses. Here is a partial list of disorders that have been associated with negative emotional states such as depression:

High blood pressure	Backaches
Asthma	Rheumatism
Dermatitis	Arthritis
Obesity	Allergies
Headaches	Peptic ulcers

Diseases that tend to be brought on by emotional states are called *psychosomatic diseases.* (*Psyche* = mind; *soma* = body. Psychosomatic diseases, therefore, are "mind-body" diseases.)

It is important to note that depression is not usually the only cause of all the above diseases. In some cases, depression may be the primary cause of the disease, but in other cases psychological factors may serve as a complication for a disease already in progress. Sometimes, depression may play only a very minor role.

But how is it possible for depression to lead to a physical disease such as arthritis? In an attempt to answer this question, some researchers have turned to experiments with animals that are thought to react in a similar manner to humans under similar circumstances. For example, one recent series of experiments conducted by the medical researcher Joseph B. Brady, which were designed to prove the relationship between psychological functioning and physical disease, used monkeys. The two monkeys were strapped into chairs, and both received electric shocks to their feet from time to time. Although the shocks were painful, they were harmless. One of the monkeys was given the opportunity to press a button when a light came on. If the monkey pressed the button in time, it and its partner would avoid the painful shock (the electricity would be cut off). The monkey with the opportunity to press the button was named the "executive monkey." The other monkey was named the "control monkey."

Remember, the control monkey had no power over the shock situation and had to suffer the consequences of the decisions made by the executive monkey. One of these monkeys developed stomach ulcers and bled to death. Which one? The answer may surprise you. It was the executive monkey, the one who had to make the decisions, that died. The monkey who suffered from psychological stress was the one who had some control over the situation—not the one who had to suffer in helpless silence.

Why did the executive monkey develop ulcers? The answer seems to be that during the periods when it was not in the decision-making chair, the executive monkey suffered from anxiety and depression. During the times when it was waiting to be placed in the executive chair—that is, during rest periods—its stomach acid increased. The acid ate away the lining of the stomach, and the monkey developed ulcers. As a consequence of the ulcers, it bled to death.

TABLE 2

BIOLOGICAL, SOCIOLOGICAL, AND PSYCHOLOGICAL FORCES

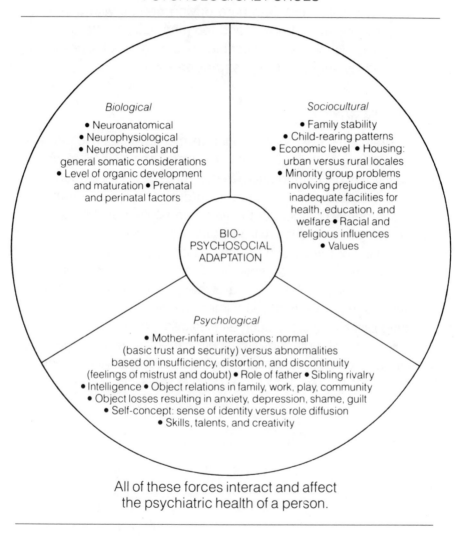

Biological

- Neuroanatomical
- Neurophysiological
- Neurochemical and general somatic considerations
- Level of organic development and maturation • Prenatal and perinatal factors

Sociocultural

- Family stability
- Child-rearing patterns
- Economic level • Housing: urban versus rural locales
- Minority group problems involving prejudice and inadequate facilities for health, education, and welfare • Racial and religious influences
- Values

BIO-PSYCHOSOCIAL ADAPTATION

Psychological

- Mother-infant interactions: normal (basic trust and security) versus abnormalities based on insufficiency, distortion, and discontinuity (feelings of mistrust and doubt) • Role of father • Sibling rivalry • Intelligence • Object relations in family, work, play, community • Object losses resulting in anxiety, depression, shame, guilt • Self-concept: sense of identity versus role diffusion • Skills, talents, and creativity

All of these forces interact and affect
the psychiatric health of a person.

(Modified after J.B. Richmond and S.L. Lustman.
J. Med. Educ. 29: 23, May 1954.)

This well-known experiment with monkeys demonstrated that emotions (in this case, anxiety and depression) can make someone ill. Scientists have evidence that human beings tend to develop ulcers the same way that the executive monkey did. The hard-driving person with unrealistic ambitions and goals, and too many difficult decisions to make, is highly susceptible to a variety of illnesses caused by stress, anxiety, and depression.

IN SUMMARY

Depression's cost to the nation in medical expenses and loss of productivity is estimated at billions of dollars annually. Yet out of ignorance, fear, or passivity, only a fraction of the sufferers will get help. Depression is a disease that more than 80 percent of the time can be successfully controlled, but countless millions suffer in silence.

Part of the reason for this is that depression is not an absolute or physically specific disease, like mumps or diabetes. It is a syndrome—a cluster of physical and emotional symptoms that sometimes masquerades as something entirely different, such as alcoholism or drug addiction. This can make diagnosis difficult, especially since experts still do not entirely agree about the nature of depression and what causes it.

CHAPTER TWO

TYPES OF DEPRESSION

_____

_____

_____

_____

_____

_____

_____

_____

_____

_____

_____

_____

It has been estimated that more than a quarter of our population suffers from depression acute enough to demand treatment, according to Nathan S. Kline, M.D., director of the Rockland Research Institute in Maryland and a leading authority on depression. This amounts to about thirty million people, making it not only the most widespread psychological disorder but also perhaps the most common of all serious medical conditions. Thus, depression may be the most underrated of all major diseases.

Many depressed patients are sad, cry frequently, and complain of feeling unhappy, or "blue." Beyond mere sadness, they may also lose the ability to feel pleasure. Pessimism about the future is another feature of depressive illness. During the sad times of life, people are generally comforted by thoughts of a happier future time. However, for many depressed people, the future looks as bleak as the past. Low self-esteem (how one looks at oneself) is a major feature of depression. Most people retain good thoughts about themselves and their personal worth even through periods of sadness, but depressed patients often deny their past achievements and feel undeserving of their current successes. This feeling of worthlessness combined with sadness robs depressed patients of their motivation to carry on with their jobs, school, friends, and even life itself. In many instances, the first sign of depression is the increasing difficulty that a person has in accomplishing everyday tasks that he or she would usually handle quite easily.

While the distinction between "normal" and "abnormal" depression is sometimes very fuzzy, any reasonable estimate would suggest that normal depressions far outnumber abnormal ones in terms of numbers of people affected at any given time. Most people suffering from normal depression will not seek nor need the specialized services of a mental health professional.

Normal depressions are almost always the result of some more or less obvious recent stress. For example, we usually think of grief as the psychological process a person goes through following the death of a loved one. Although this may be the most common and intense form of grieving, many other types of loss will give rise to a similar state in a healthy person. Loss of status or a prestigious position (either at work or in school), separation or divorce, financial loss, the break-up of a romantic affair, retirement, separation from an important friend, absence from home for the first time, or even the disappearance or death of a cherished pet may all give rise to the symptoms of acute grief.

Whatever the source, the condition has certain characteristics. The grieving person will normally "turn off" to events that would otherwise provoke a strong response; he or she will seem to retreat from life, avoiding any and all possibilities of involvement in activities, especially those associated with the loss. At the same time, the griever will often become very involved in fantasies of changing what has already happened.

The statement that time heals all does apply in some sense to the grieving process. For most people the capacity to respond to the external world is gradually regained, sadness lessens, and the person moves out again into a more productive life-style. This is the normal pattern; some people, however, seem to become stuck somewhere in the middle of the sequence, in which case they enter into a more serious psychological grieving process that might warrant intervention by a mental health specialist. In these cases the depression may have been triggered by the loss but not caused by it. Serious, prolonged depressive illnesses, such as the ones discussed in this chapter, usually have their roots in the unconscious or in some hidden physical or behavioral problem.

Depressive disorders may be episodic, occurring once or twice or at regular intervals during a person's lifetime, or they may be chronic, existing nearly all the time and requiring constant treatment and medication. Even though all depressive disorders share many of the same symptoms, there are differences that show up during diagnosis and influence treatment.

Aaron Beck, in his book *Depression: Clinical, Experimental, and Theoretical Aspects*, states that there are five basic components in a major depressive disorder: "1. A specific alteration in mood: sadness, loneliness, apathy. 2. A negative self-concept associated with self-reproaches and self-blame. 3. Regressive and self-punitive wishes: desires to escape, hide, or die. 4. Vegetative changes: anorexia [loss of appetite], insomnia, loss of libido [sex drive]. 5. Change in activity level: retardation [slowing up] or agitation."

Here, now, are the basic types of depressive disorders.

MELANCHOLIA

This type of depression is characterized by an overwhelming inability to experience pleasure, even in situations that are normally pleasurable. Melancholic individuals describe their depression, usually worse in the morning, as "different" from the sadness or grief they felt in the past, even in connection with the death of a loved one. Along with loss of pleasure and the depressed feelings, individuals with melancholia may also awaken early each morning, show a loss of appetite and weight, have excessive or exaggerated guilt feelings, and experience significant changes in normal activity levels—either becoming overactive or sluggish.

Without proper treatment, this type of depression may last for many years unchanged. In advanced stages, auditory hallucinations, usually of reproachful or accusing voices that may suggest suicide or threaten retribution, may also be experienced.

MAJOR DEPRESSIVE DISORDER

A major depressive disorder is a severe disorder that may occur in a single episode or be recurrent. Along with bipolar depression (see later in this chapter), the difficulty in treating this illness arises because the therapist is unable to tell when an "attack," or severe episode, will happen. Of the two main types of severe depression—major depressive disorder (unipolar depression, or depression only) and bipolar depression—the major depressive disorder occurs much more frequently in our society and has increased in recent years, while bipolar depression has decreased. In fact, it has been estimated that some eight to ten persons in one hundred—about twenty-five million Americans—will experience a severe depressive episode at some time in their lives. Over two million of these will suffer profound depressions (extremely deep). The great majority of identified cases occur between the ages of twenty-five and sixty-five, although such reactions may occur at any time, from early childhood to old age. The incidence of diagnosed cases is higher among females than males, with a ratio of about three to two.

There are three basic degrees of major depressive disorder.

Subacute Major Depressive Disorder
In subacute major depressive disorder, the outstanding symptoms are a loss of enthusiasm and a general slowing of mental and physical activity. The person feels dejected. Work and other activities require tremendous effort and somehow do not seem worth the bother. Feelings of unworthiness, failure, sinfulness, and guilt dominate the individual's slowed thought processes; loss of interest extends to eating and is usually reflected in a loss of weight and digestive difficulties such as constipation. Conversation is carried on in a monotone, and questions are answered with few words. In general, the person prefers just to sit alone, contemplating past problems and seeing no hope for the future. Thinking about suicide is common, and actual suicide attempts may be made.

Despite the mental and motor slowing, the person shows no actual disorientation and no real inability to think. Memory remains unimpaired, and the person is able to answer questions fairly satisfactorily if allowed sufficient time. Many of these individuals have some insight into their condition and understand that they need treatment, although they may not admit that they are depressed. Rather, they focus on physical problems such as headaches, fatigue, loss of appetite, constipation, and poor sleep.

Acute Major Depressive Disorder

In acute major depressive disorders, the mental and physical slowing down is increased. Individuals become increasingly inactive, tend to isolate themselves from others, do not speak of their own accord, and are extremely slow to respond. At times they may become quite agitated, wringing their hands, pacing, or doing other similar activities. Feelings of guilt and worthlessness increase. Patients may hold themselves responsible for problems with the world or economic depressions and may even insist that they have committed horrible sins that will bring disaster on everyone. Or they may become hypochondriacs—thinking that something is physically wrong with them when it is not.

The person experiencing acute depression sees absolutely no hope that things will ever improve. Mild to severe hallucinations and feelings of unreality may occasionally occur, particularly in connection with ideas of guilt and disease. There is considerable danger of suicide, since death generally seems the only way out for many of these people.

Depressive Stupor

When people suffer from depressive stupor, they are typically unresponsive and inactive, are often bedridden, and are usually utterly indifferent to all that goes on around them. They refuse to speak or eat and have to be tube-fed and have their elimination processes taken care of for them. Confusion concerning time, place, and other persons is extreme, and there are vivid hallucinations, often involving frightening fantasies of sin, death, and rebirth.

Fortunately, with the treatment methods available today, most depressive stupors can be rapidly reversed, and few hospitalized patients remain this severely depressed.

BIPOLAR ILLNESS
(MANIC-DEPRESSIVE REACTION)

Although it has been recognized for many years that the contrasting states of depression and elation can occur in the same patient, it was not until 1896 that the condition was designated as manic-depressive insanity. Emil Kraepelin observed the vastly opposite episodes of illness in the same individual, which he then attributed to a single disease process. In other words, at one point in the illness the person might be suicidally depressed and at another point maniacally elated.

Many patients have recurrent depressive reactions without elations; relatively few present the alternation between the two affects (way of reacting) observed by Kraepelin. This type of depression, called the manic-depressive reaction, is more commonly known today as *bipolar depression.*

Prevalence
There are striking differences in the reporting of manic-depressive illness in the various countries. The admission rates of manic-depressives to hospitals in England and Wales exceed that for the public mental hospitals in the United States by eighteen times, and by nine times when admissions in the United States are computed for both public and private mental hospitals. The recorded rate of first admissions of those with manic-depressive illness in the state of New York fell steadily from 1930 to 1950 as follows:

```
177 per 100,000 in 1920
174   "      "      "  1930
111   "      "      "  1940
 71   "      "      "  1950
```

The explanations for these differences are numerous. Probably the most widely accepted reason for the variations is the fact that nonstandardized diagnostic labeling was used. Secondly, it has been suggested that genetic differences account for higher rates in northern European countries and that the increasing immigration of southern Europeans into the United States has led to dilution of the older northern European population, with the diminished frequency of illnesses characteristic of northern populations. Thirdly, the admission rates of manic-depressive patients to private psychiatric hospitals in the United States, which cater largely to wealthier families, greatly exceed rates for the public mental hospitals, which serve the more economically deprived and largely represent waves of immigrants from southern Europe. And finally, the decline in hospital admissions of this group may rest in the increasingly successful treatment of this condition through clinic or office therapy.

The Two Sides
of Bipolar Depression
Elated mood, decreased need for sleep, increased talking, and increased social, sexual, and physical activity are typical during the manic phase. The manic person feels capable of any undertaking and tends to overlook any painful or harmful results of his or her behavior.

A person with "mixed" bipolar depression will shift back and forth from manic behavior to depressive behavior. Approximately 10 percent of all patients with depressive disorders also experience frequent episodes of mania.

The relationship between manic excitement and the despair of depression has been recognized since antiquity. Nearly two thousand years have passed since Aretaeus noted the occurrence of both extremes in the same individual, and it is little more than one hundred years since Jean-Pierre Falret, a French psychiatrist, described such mood alterations as "la folie circulaire" (periodic madness).

A manic state can be a life-threatening illness. Some patients die from physical exhaustion, dehydration, or the adverse effects of pre-existing somatic (body) conditions, such as cardiovascular disease. Others die from accidents caused by reckless behavior, and a few commit suicide.

A depressive episode may subside quite abruptly and swing right into a full-blown mania, at which time speech increases in frequency, speed, and volume, sometimes until the patient becomes hoarse. The person is constantly stimulated by new thoughts arising internally and by the external environment. It is extremely difficult to hold his or her attention long enough to obtain even the briefest answers to questions. Because of increasing carelessness and shortness of attention span, intellectual functioning is difficult to measure. Recent and past memory are also affected.

Actress Vivian Leigh suffered from bipolar depression, according to her autobiography. Dance pioneer Alvin Ailey is another widely known sufferer. At its most extreme, mixed bipolar illness torments its victims with wide, uncontrollable mood changes, from flying high and feeling like a ruler of the world to feeling low and worthless and mired in the deepest despair.

Studies have found that bipolar depression tends to run in families, and some experts believe that it may be inherited. Treatment with lithium, an antidepressant, works in most cases, but most manic-depressives must take the drug for life.

Three subcategories, or stages, are usually employed in describing behavior labeled as manic. These are hypomania, acute mania, and delirious mania. The hypomanic individual is characterized by overactivity, flightiness, and elation. It is often hard to tell the difference between hypomanic behavior and normal competitive, active, aggressive, or sociable behavior. When an individual has enormous confidence in himself or herself, undertakes many new projects at once, sleeps infrequently, makes many appointments, spends a great deal of time on the telephone, writes frequently, and generally seems involved in the world in every possible way, is he or she hypomanic or simply a hardworking, healthy, productive individual? The difference between the two people would be found in their effectiveness, consistency, and rational behavior. Hypomanic behaviors are characterized by tremendous activity, but usually very little is accomplished and others often become annoyed at the excessive behavior displayed by hypomanic individuals.

The delirious manic patient comes closest to the classic description of a raving maniac. He or she is in an extreme state of hyperactivity, is disoriented as to time and place, may hallucinate (hear or see things that are not there), be unresponsive to pain, and may pace and scream until utterly exhausted. A person may gradually progress from hypomanic to delirious mania over time, or the delirious mania may be seen, in rare instances, without any "warm-up" period.

DIAGNOSING DEPRESSION

Scientists know that there are different types of depression. Most common is what people call a real "downer," with an intense and prolonged sense of sadness, despair, guilt, and hopelessness.

TABLE 3
CLASSIC AND ATYPICAL SYMPTOMS
IN MANIC PATIENTS

Symptoms	% of Patients Manifesting Symptoms
Hyperactivity	100
Extreme Verbosity	100
Pressure of speech (talking fast)	100
Grandiosity	100
Manipulativeness	100
Irritability	100
Euphoria	90
Mood lability (mood instability)	90
Hypersexuality	80
Flight of ideas (jumping from one topic to another)	75
Delusions	75
Sexual	(25)
Persecutory	(65)
Religious	(15)
Assaultiveness or threatening behavior	75
Distractibility	70
Fear of dying	70
Intrusiveness	60
Somatic complaints	55
Some depression	55
Religiosity	50
Telephone abuse	45
Regressive behavior (urinating or defecating inappropriately; exposing self)	45
Symbolization or gesturing	40
Hallucinations (auditory and visual)	40
Confusion	35

(From Carlson, G. A., and Goodwin, F. K.
Arch Gen. Psychiatry, 28:221–228, 1973.)

TABLE 4

THE TWO SIDES OF
BIPOLAR DEPRESSION

	Manic Behavior	Depressive Behavior
Emotional Characteristics (FEELING)	elated, euphoric	gloomy, hopeless
	very sociable	socially withdrawn
	impatient	irritable
Cognitive Characteristics (THINKING)	racing thoughts, flight of ideas	slowness of thought processes
	desire for action	obsessive worrying
	impulsive behavior	inability to make decisions
	talkative	
	positive self-image	negative self-image, self-blame
	delusions of grandeur	delusions of guilt and disease
Motor Characteristics (BODY)	hyperactive	decreased motor activity
	does not become tired	always tired
	needs less sleep than usual	difficulty in sleeping
	increased sex drive	decreased sex drive
	fluctuating appetite	decreased appetite

"A depressed person isn't just down in the dumps..." said Frank Ayd, psychiatrist and research director at Taylor Manor Hospital in Maryland. "At times life may get lousy for all of us, but guilt and hopelessness are out of place."

Ninety percent of unipolar depression sufferers have a moderately severe form of the illness. This kind of depression dulls the ability to feel pleasure and causes a nagging sadness and a clinging sense of hopelessness.

A person with a depression will usually display some or all of the following symptoms, most mentioned earlier in discussing the various types of depression: He or she will be very tired all the time. Sleep will usually be off in one of two ways; either the person will go to sleep and then wake up during the night and remain awake, or else the person will sleep all the time, even during the day. The depressed person will get upset very easily over little things that ordinarily would not cause upset, will be very sad for no reason, and may even break into tears often without knowing why. Normal sex drive will be very much decreased; in fact, it will often go away altogether. A variety of physical aches and pains such as headaches will appear, and, although not very severe, will be present most of the time. The headache will usually feel like a band around the head, and the pain will tend to run down the neck, but it can occur anywhere around the head. Almost any chronic pain elsewhere, such as in the stomach or back, can be caused by depression. And these pains are not imaginary. They are quite real and often severe. The person also has difficulty enjoying things and has little enthusiasm even for things normally looked forward to, such as free time. Constipation or other digestive symptoms, such as abdominal pain or diarrhea, may occur, with a change of weight. Difficulty concentrating, making decisions, or studying may also occur, along with a feeling of worthlessness or sinfulness. In a very severe depression, there is a desire to die.

Depression attacks the whole body, and the complex of symptoms has been well documented. But a doctor who is not thinking of depression might conclude there is something physically wrong, and some depressed people receive improper treatment. "I would estimate that half of depressions are misdiagnosed," says Robert Hirschfeld, a psychiatrist and chief of the National Institute of Mental Health for the Study of Affective Disorders.

How do professionals differentiate serious clinical depression from "ordinary" unhappiness, grief, or moodiness? One sure sign is consistent, markedly exaggerated, or inappropriate responses to everyday stresses or problems plus the inability to snap back from frustration, disappointment, and loss. A sophomore in high school who falls into a deep and lingering despair over a poor grade in English is reacting in a depressive manner. If the same student had the same feelings about a serious loss, such as a death in the family, he or she would be experiencing a normal grief.

A major consideration in determining if someone has a depressive illness is that individual's ability to function in everyday life. Seriously depressed people have trouble concentrating. It takes them forever to get started in the morning. Making even the most minor decisions, such as what clothes to put on, can be agonizing. Unrelieved feelings of sorrow, helplessness, and hopelessness, which are often joined with acute anxiety, frequently drive the depression sufferer to seek medical help. Each day, each hour, is torment. Less severely depressed individuals can experience the same symptoms but less intensely.

When psychologists and psychiatrists make a diagnosis of depression, they are stating that the depressive behavior is not normal. The following chart, taken from the work of Dr. Aaron Beck, shows the changes from normal to depressed.

TABLE 5

CHANGES FROM A NORMAL
TO A DEPRESSED STATE

Items	Normal State	Depressed State
STIMULUS		RESPONSE
Loved object	Affection	Loss of feeling, revulsion
Favorite activities	Pleasure	Boredom
New opportunities	Enthusiasm	Indifference
Humor	Amusement	Mirthlessness
Novel stimuli	Curiosity	Lack of interest
Abuse	Anger	Self-criticism, sadness
GOAL OR DRIVE		DIRECTION
Gratification	Pleasure	Avoidance
Welfare	Self-care	Self-neglect
Self-preservation	Survival	Suicide
Achievement	Success	Withdrawal
THINKING		APPRAISAL
About self	Realistic	Self-devaluating
About future	Hopeful	Hopeless
About environment	Realistic	Overwhelming
BIOLOGICAL AND PHYSIOLOGICAL ACTIVITIES		SYMPTOM
Appetite	Spontaneous hunger	Loss of appetite
Sexuality	Spontaneous desire	Loss of desire
Sleep	Restful	Disturbed
Energy	Spontaneous	Fatigued

The *DSM III (Diagnostic and Statistical Manual of Mental Disorders, Third Edition)* of the American Psychiatric Association is used by most therapists to help make the diagnosis of a major (severe) depressive episode.

TESTS TO DIAGNOSE DEPRESSION

Observing a person's behavior, interviewing parents and friends, and talking to the depressed person are the standard methods of determining a diagnosis of depression. Psychologists and psychiatrists may also use certain tests, administered orally, to help them. These tests are not pass-or-fail but are called "personality inventories." Aaron Beck has created a depression inventory based upon his scientific research. This inventory may be used to help determine the type and severity of the depression.

The instructions and a few sample questions from Beck's depression inventory are shown below. (Please do not write in this book.)

Instructions

This is a questionnaire. On the questionnaire are groups of statements. Please read the entire group of statements in each category. Then pick out the one statement in the group which best describes the way you feel today, that is, right now! Circle the number beside the statement you have chosen. If several statements in the group seem to apply equally well, circle each one.

Be sure to read all statements in each group before making your choice.

(SADNESS)
0   I do not feel sad
1   I feel blue or sad
2   I am blue or sad all the time and I can't snap
    out of it
3   I am so sad or unhappy that I can't stand it

(SELF-DISLIKE)
0   I don't feel disappointed in myself
1a I am disappointed in myself
1b I don't like myself
2   I am disgusted with myself
3   I hate myself

(CRYING)
0   I don't cry any more than usual
1   I cry more now than I used to
2   I cry all the time now. I can't stop it
3   I used to be able to cry but now I can't cry
    at all even though I want to

(WORK RETARDATION)
0   I can work about as well as before
1a It takes extra effort to get started at doing
    something
1b I don't work as well as I used to
2   I have to push myself very hard to do anything
3   I can't do any work at all

Projective tests try to elicit responses that will reveal a person's underlying feelings and personality traits, which in turn can help the therapist make an accurate diagnosis. The tests have the person perform relatively simple tasks, some requiring imagination, such as drawing pictures, making up sentences, finding shapes in ink blots, or making up stories from sketchy information provided to them. These tests have been administered to large numbers of people with and without emotional disorders, and the scales used to interpret the test results are based on statistical information from previous testings. Following are some of the most widely used projective tests.

The Rorschach Ink Blot Test

The Rorschach Ink Blot Test was developed by Swiss psychiatrist Herman Rorschach in the early 1920s. The test consists of ten cards with ink blots, half colored and half in shades of black and white. The ten cards are presented to an individual in standard sequence, and the examiner notes the reactions of the person, the way in which he or she turns the cards, the time taken before responding, and the exact verbal content of all responses. After the person has described what he or she sees in the ink blots, the therapist will ask questions about particular responses that were made. Interpretation of the responses is very complicated, and a therapist needs extensive training to become proficient at this type of projective testing. At the present time there is some disagreement regarding the validity of Rorschach's ink blots as perceptual indicators of personality.

The Thematic Apperception Test

The Thematic Apperception Test (TAT), developed by Henry Murray in 1935, consists of thirty pictures and one blank card. The pictures show people engaged in a variety of activities that could be thought of as dramatic situations. The cards are presented one at a time. The person being tested is asked to make up a story describing the scene in each picture, the events leading up to that scene, and the events that will grow out of it. He or she is also asked to describe the thoughts and feelings of the people in the story. When the TAT story is interpreted, the therapist usually tries to determine who is the hero, that is, the character with whom the person seems to have identified. Some psychotherapists use TAT responses as clues to find hidden problem areas that may eventually lead to depression.

Children's Apperception Test

The Children's Apperception Test (CAT) was introduced by Leopold Bellak in 1949 for use with children between the ages of three and ten. Instead of using humans as the central characters on the cards, the test uses animal characters and may give the therapist insights and helpful information about a child's self-concept and his or her relationships with others.

The MMPI

Probably the most popular personality test for the diagnosis of depression is the Minnesota Multiphasic Personality Inventory (MMPI). Research leading to the development of the MMPI began about 1939. Starke R. Hathaway, a psychologist, and J. Charnley McKinley, a neuropsychiatrist, originally developed the test to evaluate individuals exhibiting some signs of psychopathology and to make predictions concerning their potential responses to treatment.

A sample of more than one thousand items was assembled from books on psychiatry, case histories, existing attitude scales, and the authors' clinical experience. An attempt was made to draw conclusions about symptoms, attitudes, actions, and likely indicators of personality maladjustment. All of the items were tested on a number of persons corresponding in age, sex, and education to the population of Minnesota in the 1930 census, and their responses were compared with a number of hospitalized groups showing specific patterns of maladjustment. The normal group included 724 people visiting patients at the University of Minnesota Hospital, smaller groups of medical students, normal clients from a testing bureau, and 265 Minneapolis-St. Paul-area government workers.

Since the early days of the MMPI, the number of test questions and the amount of information pertaining to the results have been greatly increased. Information regarding results is constantly being updated.

WHO TAKES THE MMPI?   A test taker sixteen years of age or older with at least six years of successful schooling should be able to complete the MMPI without difficulty. At the present time there is some discussion about different scores obtained from various ethnic and subculture groups. The test usually takes from sixty minutes to several hours to complete.

The MMPI has been employed as a screening device for personality problems in a wide range of mental patients, for personnel selection by government agencies and industry, and in hundreds of research studies. The MMPI has even been the subject of inquiry at congressional hearings investigating the use of psychological tests in selecting Peace Corps candidates.

Like the other personality tests, the MMPI is only one tool in helping to discover the inner feelings and emotions of an individual. Results obtained from this test are almost always evaluated along with personal observations and interviews conducted by the therapist.

SAMPLE MMPI QUESTIONS   The MMPI consists of 566 true or false questions. Here is a sampling of some questions taken directly from the MMPI form.

44. Much of the time my head seems to hurt all over.
121. I believe I am being plotted against.
138. Criticism or scolding hurts me terribly.
207. I enjoy many different kinds of play and recreation.
252. No one cares much what happens to me.
301. Life is a strain for me much of the time.
337. I feel anxiety about something or someone almost all the time.
360. Almost every day something happens to frighten me.
379. I very seldom have spells of the blues.
418. At times I think I am no good at all.
451. My worries seem to disappear when I get into a crowd of lively friends.

THE DEPRESSION SCALE   The score a person achieves on the MMPI "D" (depression) scale will tell the therapist whether the person feels generally cheerful, enthusiastic, optimistic, lively, alert, and outgoing, or pessimistic, withdrawn, evasive, and plagued by worry. The depression scale is compared with other scales on the test, and an overall interpretation of the test results is developed by the therapist. Learning to correctly interpret the results of the MMPI (or any personality or projective test) takes specialized training and extensive practice.

CHAPTER THREE

HOW WE BECOME
DEPRESSED

_____

_____

_____

_____

_____

_____

CASE ONE

Karen had just spent the last twenty minutes arguing with her mother. How could her parents be so unreasonable, she thought. To be asked on a date by a junior, and such a popular one, was something most freshman girls could only hope for. But her parents had said no, and even a quiet talk with her mother had not improved the situation any. There seemed no way of convincing her parents to let her go to the drive-in movie with Chris on Friday night. Karen sat in her room, not knowing what to do next. Her anger was soon replaced by a feeling of hopelessness and frustration. She lost her appetite, and by dinnertime all she wanted to do was to get into bed, pull the covers over her head, and go to sleep. Even calling her best friend, Mary Kay, held no interest for her tonight. She just sat in the chair by her desk, not really listening to the rock music on the radio but staring off into space as she scribbled on a piece of paper in front of her.

Tom heard the awful screech of tires on the street all the way from his backyard. He immediately looked for his dog. Prince had been there only a few minutes before, running and chasing him around the yard. Prince had been his birthday present six months ago, and ever since that time the two of them had been almost inseparable.

Tom ran around the side of the house. As he came into the front yard, he saw the car stopped and the distraught driver looking under the front bumper. Although he couldn't bring himself to look, Tom knew his dog was dead.

For a week after Prince's death, Tom didn't feel like eating much, and sometimes dreams of Prince would awaken him in the night and he would cry softly so that no one would hear. A book report had been due in school two days ago, but he didn't care and just couldn't seem to get to work on it. His parents offered to buy him a new dog, but the hurt was still too strong.

Tom was depressed, and nothing anybody did or said seemed to help. Two weeks after the death of Prince, Tom noticed that he wasn't thinking about the dog as much as before. He would feel hungry, and his eating returned to normal. Missed homework assignments were made up. When Tom told his parents he'd like to get another dog, they were overjoyed.

CASE THREE

As long as Sherry could remember, her mother had been depressed. Her mother never called it depression but would always say she felt "down," and whenever Sherry asked her what was wrong, the answer would always be, "There's nothing really wrong." But Sherry knew there was something wrong. Her mother always seemed to be going to the doctor, and at least several times a week Sherry's father would say, "Now, let's not have any problems because your mother's not feeling well, and we don't want to disturb her." When Sherry did do something wrong, she noticed that her mother would become very angry at first, yelling and screaming; then suddenly she would become very quiet and wouldn't talk to Sherry for hours. There just didn't seem to be any way for Sherry to please her mother.

Her mother's behavior remained a mystery to Sherry as she grew up. More than once, in the midst of an argument, a friend or relative might say, "You're acting just like your mother." After one occasion, when a very close friend made a similar comment to her, she became angry at first, then realized that in many ways her behavior was like her mother's, especially when she became frustrated or failed at something.

CASE FOUR

"Sometimes I think everyone would be better off if I were dead," sobbed Helen. Nothing seemed to be going right. Her grades in school disappointed her parents. Her boyfriend had recently broken up with her to go with a girl from another school—a girl who had been her best friend! Sneaking wine from her parents' liquor cabinet didn't seem to help like it had in the past, and now, although she was sneaking drinks of wine every day, there was still a feeling of worthlessness. Her face was broken out worse than usual, and she felt sure that everyone must be staring at her pimples. She had no friends. Her parents spent most of their time yelling at her or criticizing her. She felt lonely and isolated.

Here are just a few of the reasons that may cause people to become depressed:

> Genetic cause
> Change
> Alcohol or drugs
> Reaction to loss
> Not meeting the expectations of others
> Disappointment
> Postpartum depression
> Hormonal or other chemical causes

What causes severe depression and makes it so widespread and long lasting? Why do people consume millions of tranquilizers and antidepressants yearly? Why do they seek out help from psychiatrists, psychologists, and counselors or join therapy groups? The answers are as numerous as the problems. An unhappy childhood or an inherited tendency toward worry; a poor diet; low blood sugar; and the normal traumas of life such as a broken relationship, failure at work, failure at school, or the loss of a loved one are just a few of the possible causes. Most depressions are triggered by one or a combination of stresses, but, unfortunately, depression does not always disappear when the stress goes away. Some depressions seem to have no outside cause at all.

DEPRESSION CAUSED
BY OBJECT LOSS

In depression, the element of loss is always of great importance. The loss may be obvious, recent, and real, as in normal grief; or it may have occurred in the past and never been properly experienced, as in delayed grief and depressive guilt reactions.

Object losses at certain phases of development can be related to depression in later life, but this relationship is not always a simple one to determine. Many people who have suffered severe losses at crucial periods in their development have few or no problems, whereas others who have suffered relatively minor losses develop severe depression. In working with a depressed person, the therapist may try to establish the relationship between early object loss and the present illness, thus providing a valuable guide for treatment. In addition, it is the responsibility of the therapist to help define object loss and to help the patient resolve any feelings or emotions that may have led to depression.

The kind of parenting received in the early stages of development is of great importance. Some parents are naturally confident and loving, whereas others have unending difficulties. A close and supportive relationship with the mother, particularly in the first year, is believed by many to enable the child to form relationships with others later in life. If the infant is denied the advantage of a close and affectionate relationship with its mother, the person may remain aloof and standoffish later, unable to form intimate and lasting relationships. Because of this fact, it is extremely important that institutionalized children be provided not only with proper physical care but also with adequate emotional mothering.

A developmental phase in infancy is that of self-object differentiation—knowing and realizing the difference between oneself and various objects. Sooner or later each child discovers that its mother is not there all the time and that this means it is separate from its mother and from the outside world. At this point in the child's development, the child learns to say "I," and self-assertiveness begins. It is extremely important for parents to help their child begin to develop its own separate identity.

If the absence of one parent occurs later in the child's development, the possibility of depression is increased.

STRESS AND DEPRESSION

Stress is something that all of us experience throughout our lives. It may help us get a report finished or provide that last-minute boost of energy to study for a test. But it may also occur when a person faces a threatening or unfamiliar situation (real or imagined) and may lead directly to feelings of depression. Situations found to cause stress include illness, loss of a job, promotion in a job, and even marriage. During the first stages of a stress response, a person's strength and energy may increase temporarily. The body's defenses against disease are also activated, thus preparing the person for the stressful event.

When stress occurs over a short period of time or only occasionally, the body will usually respond in a healthy way. But when stress continues for weeks, months, or even years, it may result in damage to certain parts of the body and reduce bodily defenses, allowing disease to take root.

When a person is under chronic (prolonged) stress, he or she may become severely depressed. Chronic stress and depression often seem to go hand-in-hand.

Any cause of stress is called a stressor. Stressors include illness, which forces the body to activate its defenses against disease; injury; and even annoying or hazardous environmental conditions such as constant noise, extreme heat, or extreme cold. Stress may also occur when a person has to adapt to an unfamiliar situation such as a change of job, a change of home, going to a new school, the addition of a new member to the family, such as the birth of a baby, or the death of a close relative or family member. Changes in a person's diet may also trigger stress.

Each person's individual reaction to stressors is different, and what is stressful to one person may not be to another. Studies have shown that if a person is in good physical condition, his or her ability to deal with stress is increased.

Understanding how stress affects your body, learning methods to cope with it, and planning for possible stressors in the future all decrease the chances that stress will become chronic and lead to depression.

How Stress Affects the Body

There are few parts of the body that the stress reaction does not affect. When a stress reaction occurs within the body, several physical changes occur, usually within seconds, their sequence and activity started automatically by the body. All of these actions are the body's way of protecting itself against a real or imagined stressor.

A part of the brain called the hypothalamus regulates the body's responses to stressors. Neural or chemical signals alert the hypothalamus when a stressor is at work. The hypothalamus then sends chemical signals to the pituitary gland, which, in turn, sends ACTH hormone down to the adrenal glands resting above the kidneys. The outer layer, or cortex, of each adrenal gland secretes cortical steroids, which flow through the glands' inner core, or medula, and, activating the nervous system, set off a lightning-fast outpouring of adrenaline into the bloodstream. Now the blood vessels of the skin contract, and blood is forced away from the extremities (arms and legs) and into the muscles and vital organs. The heartbeat increases. Blood pressure rises. At the same time, adrenaline causes the liver to convert stored glycogen into active blood sugar (glucose) for fueling nerve and muscle cells with extra energy. Simultaneously, still more adrenaline dilates the bronchi so as to allow maximum intake of oxygen for the blood; dilates the pupils of the eyes; contracts the spleen, forcing out its reserve supply of red blood cells; activates chemicals for coagulation of the blood in the event of upcoming injury; and heightens the tautness of all voluntary muscles.

Stress-Related Illnesses

Prolonged stress may temporarily interfere with the body's physical ability to maintain enough energy to resist disease. As a result, a person may feel extremely fatigued and be unable to fight illness. Long-term stress can also affect the skin and internal membranes. Rashes, ulcers, or other disorders of the skin, stomach, or intestines may result. Other conditions associated with stress include high blood pressure and long-term malfunctioning of glands such as the adrenals, pancreas, pituitary, and thyroid. Extremely prolonged and severe stress can lead to potentially fatal illnesses, such as heart problems, and to severe depression.

A Direct Connection
Between
Stress and Depression

Serotonin, a neurochemical, when existing in proper proportions within the brain, works to prevent depression and insomnia. During excessive stress, there is an extra production of hormones that may prevent the brain from providing an adequate supply of serotonin. The well-known pediatrician Dr. Lendon H. Smith has stated that an amino acid called tryptophan, found in beef and other protein-rich foods, is important in allowing the body to produce enough serotonin for the prevention of depression and to ensure proper sleep.

Frequently, scientists do not agree as to the cause of a particular emotional problem, but in the case of stress-induced depression there is a high degree of agreement.

TABLE 6

STRESSORS PRECEDING
SEVERE DEPRESSION

Stressful Event	Patients Affected (from total of 40)

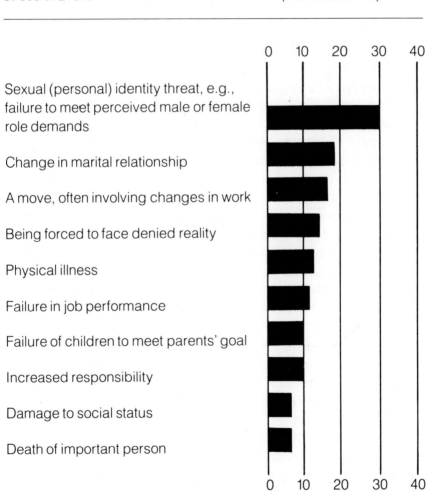

Sexual (personal) identity threat, e.g., failure to meet perceived male or female role demands

Change in marital relationship

A move, often involving changes in work

Being forced to face denied reality

Physical illness

Failure in job performance

Failure of children to meet parents' goal

Increased responsibility

Damage to social status

Death of important person

In an intense study of forty depressed patients conducted in 1970, Leff, Roatch, and Bunney found that each patient had been subjected to multiple stressful events prior to early symptoms and to a clustering of such events during the month preceding the actual breakdown in functioning. The chart on page 61 shows the ten types of stressors most frequently involved.

GENETIC CAUSES OF DEPRESSION

The rather common occurrence of depressive illness in the same family suggests that genetics may be a contributing cause, but this is difficult to prove. Data accumulated in recent studies strongly suggest that a genetic component may be especially significant in the occurrence of manic-depressive illness. Scientists have stated that the incidence of manic-depressive illness is twenty-five times as high among siblings (brothers and sisters) as in the average population. If it occurs in identical twins, both of them will be affected in more than half the cases.

In a German psychiatric clinic to which patients were admitted irrespective of social position, doctors found manic-depressive illness to be nearly three times as frequent in the highest social class and four times as frequent in the professional classes as in the general population. This distribution of illness seems to be similar to that observed by American psychiatrists. In World War II, manic-depressive patients in the U.S. Army were three times as frequent among officers as among enlisted men.

In 1975, in the *American Journal of Psychiatry*, Dr. Larry Pardue presented startling evidence that certain forms of depression may be passed from parents to their children through genes. A recent study reported in the *New England Journal of Medicine* said that a gene or genes apparently linked to depression had been located on the sixth chromosome. This discovery was made by Lowell Weitkamp, a geneticist at the University of Rochester in New York. Through the analysis of blood samples Weitkamp's analysis showed a genetic pattern.

While the scientific world continues its search for a genetic link to depression, other geneticists remain skeptical. Dr. Elliot Gershon, chief of the psychogenetics section of the National Institute of Mental Health, questions Weitkamp's findings, stating that he doubts that the specific genetic link to depression has been discovered. If such a gene can be found, however, researchers say that it may be possible for doctors to screen couples who are likely to have children prone to depression.

New and exciting advances are being made in genetic research, and someday scientists may discover exactly how genetics and depression are linked. If detection of a depression gene were possible, then scientists might be able to do something to alter the situation even before the baby is born.

BIOCHEMICAL FACTORS
IN CAUSING DEPRESSION

In 1899, Kraepelin stated that manic-depressive disorders were due to toxic substances in the body. Since that time much research has been directed toward finding a possible chemical reason within the body for depressive illness. Since the 1960s the "catecholamine hypothesis" has related both mania and depression to the level of catecholamines (brain chemicals) in the brain.

The nervous system of the body acts like a giant electrical complex, with many switches and relays. These brain chemicals, known as biogenic amines, serve as neural transmitters and regulate the extent to which nerve impulses are carried across the synapses from one neuron to the next. The biogenic amines help to either open or close the relays, thus preventing or helping messages go from one part of the brain to another or from the brain to other parts of the body. Evidence now suggests that various physical therapies often used to treat severe depression—such as electroconvulsive therapy, potent antidepressive drugs, and lithium carbonate—affect the functioning of certain biogenic amines in the brain. This, in turn, would affect the transmission of nerve impulses within the brain. One of the catecholamines, norepinephrine, has been found to play an especially important role in the biochemistry of severe depression. For a time it was thought that mania and depression were due simply to an excess or deficiency of norepinephrine, but we now know that the situation is much more complex than this. Another drug produced naturally in the brain, serotonin, also appears to play a significant role in relieving depression or actually preventing it.

CHANGE AS A
CAUSE OF DEPRESSION

Feelings of depression may be caused by holidays, moving, or a change in school or job. For most people, such changes usually cause only a temporary sadness or empty feeling that disappears after adjustments are made. But for some people, the feelings of depression may last for months, even years.

Here, now, are some of the types of changes that can lead to depression:

>Divorce
>Change of job
>Loss of job
>Change of school

Financial problems
Change in family structure
Physical change due to accident or illness
Change in interpersonal relationships

ALCOHOL AND DRUGS

Alcohol as a major factor in depression cannot be overlooked. There are estimated to be more than five million alcoholics in the United States and many more millions who use alcohol excessively and who contribute to the widespread problem of alcohol abuse.

One-third to one-half of those attempting suicide have consumed alcohol a short time before their attempt. The abuse of alcohol and other drugs may be the most widespread social problem in our society, with its most serious outcome possibly being depression that leads to loss of life.

The number of young people between the ages of eight and eighteen who use alcohol and could be classified as alcoholics has increased at an alarming rate in recent years. The abuse of prescription and nonprescription drugs has also skyrocketed over the past ten years. Alcohol and drugs may frequently be used to try to relieve the symptoms of depression, but this is always a dead-end street. Many drugs, including alcohol, can actually intensify and deepen the depression. In fact, mixing alcohol and other drugs may give a person the opposite of the desired effect and can lead to death. Some people commit suicide by deliberately misusing drugs or mixing them with alcohol. For example, in fatalities associated with propoxyphene (a painkiller), as many as 80 percent may be suicides. A recent ten-year review of the Dade County (Miami), Florida, medical examiner's records related to propoxyphene overdose indicated a 76 percent incidence of suicide.

REACTION TO LOSS

Another kind of depression is the sadness that comes from the death of someone close or the end of a close relationship.

After the death of a close relative or friend, most people experience what is called a grief reaction. This is entirely normal. In fact, not showing the grief reaction may be considered abnormal behavior. Common features of the grief reaction include:

Physical distress causing the urge to sigh frequently
Tightness of the throat
An empty feeling in the stomach
A feeling of weakness
A feeling of tiredness
A lack of interest in normal activities

In addition to these reactions there may be a preoccupation with thinking about the dead person, guilt, hostility, and disturbing dreams. In most cases, the grief reaction will pass with time, but it may make the person more susceptible to a continuing depression. Some doctors feel that people who have experienced the death of a loved one may have increased vulnerability to depression for as long as two years.

Grieving children and adolescents may fantasize about the return of a deceased parent, while others express suicidal thoughts, with a wish to try to join the dead parent. Guilt is a very common experience, especially when the relationship with the parent was poor or mixed with anger and confusion. At times the mourning person may feel responsible for the death, especially if in anger he or she recently wished the parent dead. Doctors find that the loss of a parent during childhood seems to increase the chances for depression when one becomes an adult.

Loss of a parent through separation or divorce, removal to or from a foster home, or even rejection within an intact family may cause feelings of grief, anger, and, at times, depression. Children may interpret the separation of parents as an act directed toward them. Some children even feel responsible for their parents' separation and will make desperate efforts to reunite them. If these efforts are unsuccessful, depression may set in and could last for a long time.

Children who move around from foster home to foster home may experience repeated feelings of abandonment that become overwhelming and cause extreme depression that can last for years. The children feel that no one loves them, and they become very sad and withdrawn.

Children who have been adopted or who live with a stepparent may often experience similar feelings related to the fear of abandonment. When they don't know how to express these fears, they may retreat into depression.

NOT MEETING EXPECTATIONS

Children may be extremely self-critical, often finding fault with themselves. They are always looking for models to imitate, and the goals they set for themselves or goals set for them by others are often unrealistically high. Undue pressure can come from teachers, TV, magazines and books, and parents. It is not uncommon for parents to want a son or daughter to achieve things they could not when they were their child's age. Constant pushing may cause an adolescent to become depressed. Many times, receiving a failing grade, the breaking up of a friendship, or failing in sports may lead to a self-inflicted depression, and a loss of approval by parents, teachers, or friends can deepen the depression. When children feel that no one approves of them or likes them, they begin to not like themselves.

POSTPARTUM DEPRESSION
(DEPRESSION
FOLLOWING CHILDBIRTH)

Postpartum depression, or "baby blues," is rapidly being acknowledged by doctors as a common aftereffect of childbirth. Though its intensity ranges from mild anxiety to severe depression, most women will experience depression of some kind after a child is born.

Women who are ill-prepared for motherhood, fearful of failure, or very uneasy about assuming the responsibility of bringing up a child seem to be inclined to suffer from severe postpartum depression. Some may want the child but at the same time see it as an obstacle to freedom or a serious block in their pursuit of a career.

Almost every new mother goes through a low period that begins about three days after the birth of her child. This often coincides with when it is time to leave the hospital. The down feeling may last only a few days, but if a woman is physically run down or generally more susceptible to depression, the feeling may persist for weeks, even months. Among the feelings most commonly experienced during postpartum depression are confusion, shock, insecurity, inadequacy, fear, an inability to cope with the baby, and disappointment about its sex or appearance. Many doctors attribute postpartum depression to a hormonal imbalance following childbirth, but the evidence is still inconclusive, since depression has been noted in adoptive as well as natural mothers.

Some physicians prescribe drugs to help a woman who is in a severe depressive state, but usually it is preferable to just offer emotional support and wait until the episode passes. If the mother receives support and reassurance from her family, friends, and other mothers, the chances of a rapid and complete recovery from postpartum depression are excellent.

HORMONAL CAUSES
OF DEPRESSION

What about hormonal imbalances? Hormonal changes during a woman's menstrual cycle or as a result of using oral contraceptives seem to be associated with feelings of depression, but differences in mood are small, and research findings are thus far inconclusive. The greater-than-normal risk for depression after the birth of a child, as we have just seen, has been related to a hormonal imbalance. Depression at menopause is presently being studied at numerous research centers.

Dr. Robert Greenblatt, a professor at the Medical College of Georgia and an authority on endocrinology, believes that hormone therapy can be a significant help in treating postmenopausal depression. There is a great deal of anxiety at this time of life, which often coincides with the last child leaving home. The so-called empty-nest syndrome can result. Many women respond to large doses of pure, nonsynthetic estrogen and experience dramatic relief from depression, just as large doses of testosterone can be effective in treating male depression at this time of life.

LEARNED HELPLESSNESS

Another approach to defining the reasons why someone may become depressed is taken by Martin Seligman. Seligman's research has stimulated a good deal of controversy. The central concept for his theory was developed from laboratory experiments with dogs. During these experiments the dogs were given a series of electrical shocks and were not allowed to escape. They would struggle at first but eventually would give up, lie helpless, and endure the discomfort. Later, when escape was possible, the dogs continued to passively endure the shocks. They had learned to become helpless. When researchers took other dogs and allowed them to escape when first shocked, the dogs quickly learned to avoid or escape additional shocks. Seligman hypothesized that depression in humans may represent a state of learned helplessness. He further observed that people who are depressed often think they have no control over their environment and passively endure problems that they are actually able to avoid.

Recently Seligman has refined his theory to distinguish between universal helplessness and personal helplessness. Universal helplessness is experienced when a situation cannot be changed by an individual, no matter how competent he or she is. An example of this would be the depression experienced by a mother whose child is dying of an incurable disease. Obviously, there is nothing that she could do to reverse the effects of the disease. In personal helplessness, an individual may become severely depressed in a situation over which he or she could have some control. In other words, almost all people experience helplessness in certain uncontrollable situations, but only some people experience helplessness in other, more manageable situations. One student receives a failing grade mid-year and gives up all hope of achieving a good grade by the end of the year in that class, whereas another student who receives a failing grade gets help from tutors, studies harder, and is able to raise the grade. People who suffer from a sense of personal helplessness are more prone to fall into depression.

The learned-helplessness theory of depression is probably only one factor that should be considered along with chemical states, physiological conditions, genetics, stress, and environmental change. Through his theory of learned helplessness, though, Seligman has come up with suggestions for treatment strategies to help the depressed person; these will be discussed in detail in Chapter Five.

CHAPTER FOUR

DEPRESSION
AND SUICIDE

_____

_____

_____

_____

_____

_____

_____

_____

_____

_____

_____

_____

The desire to commit suicide is the most serious complication of depressive disorders. Feelings of worthlessness and guilt overcome the individual, and he or she feels unfit to live. Sometimes these feelings remain just thoughts; other times they lead to suicide attempts.

Not all those suffering from depressive disorders attempt suicide, nor are all those who attempt suicide suffering from a depressive disorder. It is estimated that 15 percent of depressed persons eventually commit suicide. Other studies indicate that a person hospitalized for depression at some time in his or her life is about thirty times more likely to commit suicide than is the nondepressed person, with the greatest risk during or immediately following hospitalization.

The possibility of suicide increases with advancing age. In recent years, moreover, there have been alarming increases in suicide among young adults and adolescents. Nearly twice as many women attempt suicide, but three times as many men as women are successful in the attempt.

Doctors and scientists are extremely concerned about the drastic increase in the number of children and young adults who commit suicide each year. Officials say that there are at least twice as many unreported youth suicides as reported ones. The unreported ones are frequently hidden by parents or disguised as accidents.

Studies of youthful victims who died by their own hand show that only a small proportion are psychotic (severely mentally ill) or medically insane. Most of them suffer from loneliness or feelings of hopelessness or despair. Most of these youthful victims were torn between wanting to live and the feeling that they had nothing to live for.

In the United States, suicide is the ninth most common cause of death, according to the National Center for Health Statistics. In comparison, homicides are the twelfth ranking cause of death.

The Golden Gate Bridge in San Francisco is at present the number one suicide location of the world. In its first forty-one years of existence, there have been official reports of 625 suicide-deaths and perhaps two hundred additional deaths that have escaped notice. Many other suicide attractors—the Eiffel Tower, the Arroyo Secco Bridge of Pasadena, California, and the Mount Mihara volcano in Japan—have had safety structures built to prevent additional suicide attempts. The proposal to build such a suicide barrier on the Golden Gate Bridge has been debated for more than thirty years. No action has been taken because of the high cost and the fact that many people believe that those who are prevented from jumping off the bridge will simply find another way to kill themselves.

Although the rate for older people committing suicide has dropped slightly in recent years, figures from the Los Angeles Suicide Prevention Center show that the rate among young people in Los Angeles more than doubled in the years between 1960 and 1970. At Yale-New Haven

TABLE 7

SUICIDE RATES PER 100,000
POPULATION, ANNUALLY

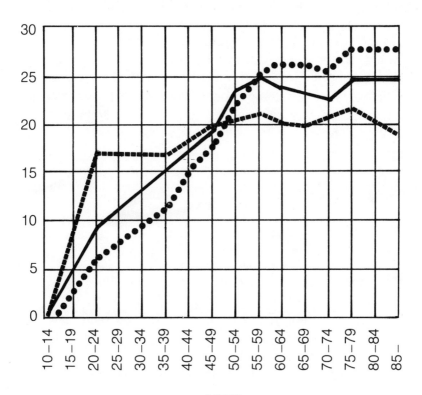

AGES

●●●●● 1955
———— 1965
■■■■■■■■ 1975

Rates of suicide for different age groups in 1955, 1965, and 1975.
Note the dramatic increase in suicides in the 10–24 age groups and
the decrease in the age groups over age 45.

Hospital, the number of persons admitted for unsuccessful suicide attempts has increased elevenfold since 1955, and most of these "attempters" are under thirty.

To summarize, there are between 25,000 and 40,000 suicides in the United States annually, with approximately ten times as many suicide attempts. In the fifteen-to-thirty-four-year-old population, suicide is the second leading cause of death in men and the third leading cause of death in women. A completed suicide occurs every twenty-six minutes, and a suicide attempt is made every 2.5 minutes. It is shocking to note that in most cases of a completed suicide or suicide attempt, the person could be seen to have symptoms of depression and, if properly treated, might have been prevented from taking the action.

DEPRESSION
LEADING TO SUICIDE

Depression can lead to suicide whenever:

> The present looks bleak and the future seems
> hopeless.
> The feelings of worthlessness and hopelessness
> are so great that "everybody would be better
> off if I were dead."
> The person's mood is so intense that reassurance
> by family, physician, or friends does not help.

Physical or emotional signs of a person who may be suicidal can include:

> Poor posture, suggesting fatigue or dejection
> Sad facial expression
> Slowed speech, with voice low and monotonous
> Dulled, slowed thinking

Agitation or anxiety present with depression

Poor appetite

Sleep problems; trouble going to sleep and waking early

Energy level low

Alcohol use increases

Increase in use of prescription or illegal drugs

Behavioral changes; in young people may include truancy, hostility, antisocial acts, sudden decline in school performance, difficulty in concentrating, loss of interest in recreational activities

But perhaps the best indication that a depressed person may attempt suicide is communication of a suicide intent. Few people attempt suicide without signaling their intent to someone. Another very important danger signal is an unsuccessful suicide attempt in the past.

USE OF ANTIDEPRESSANT DRUGS IN THE TREATMENT OF SUICIDAL PATIENTS

Extreme caution must always be exercised in prescribing antidepressant drugs for suicidal persons. When taken with alcohol, death can easily result from overdose. Also, a person using these drugs can experience side effects such as feelings of confusion, restlessness, or loss of control. Persons with a past history of psychosis or symptoms of "borderline psychosis" can have very serious side effects from antidepressants, such as the triggering of a psychotic episode.

Another problem with antidepressant drugs is that it takes ten to fourteen days before there is any noticeable lifting of depression, even though the person may be sleeping better during this time as a result of a sedative (quieting) side effect. This delayed drug action must be explained very carefully to the patient, because most people expect to feel better immediately after taking a drug.

Another danger of suicide during a drug-treatment program occurs after the depression lifts. Some depression victims are so physically slowed down that they do not have the energy to carry out a suicide plan. When they begin to feel better, they may put their plan into effect. Because of this, it is preferable to use antidepressant drugs in combination with psychiatric hospitalization for a depressed person who is highly suicidal, especially if he or she spends a great deal of time alone.

Therapists who deal with crisis situations must never lose sight of the fact that antidepressants are not emergency drugs. Most mental health professionals believe that the prescription of any drug as a substitute for effective crisis counseling is irresponsible. Not only can drug use precipitate a suicide, but the unwarranted prescription of drugs may also lead to serious drug abuse problems.

CHAPTER FIVE

TREATMENTS AND THERAPIES

_____

_____

_____

_____

_____

_____

_____

_____

_____

_____

_____

_____

There are almost as many different types of therapy for depression as there are causes of depression. One of the most difficult choices a depression sufferer has to make can be what type of therapy would be best for him or her.

According to the American Psychiatric Association, depression has become the most common form of mental disorder. While everyone feels sad now and then, depression can be serious. Every year doctors treat four to eight million Americans for depression, about 250,000 of whom require hospitalization. Many more never find their way to a doctor.

Although sadness is a common emotion in everyone's life, acute and chronic (long-lasting) depression represents a serious human illness that has become so prevalent that our time may be known as the "decade of depression." Indeed, depression has become a household word.

Yet, even with increasing numbers of people reporting depression, these disorders are among the most responsive to treatment. Advances in therapy have helped to alleviate and minimize the symptoms and mood complications of depression, enabling persons to live normal lives. A variety of treatments are available, and the type chosen depends on many factors, including the patient's overall condition, the diagnosis, and the patient's personality. The three basic types of treatment—psychological therapy (individual and group), electroshock therapy, and drug therapy—may be used singly or in combination. Other types of therapy include exercise and nutritional therapy.

PSYCHOLOGICAL THERAPY

The term *psychological* or *psychiatric therapy* can apply to individual, group, or in-patient hospitalization therapies and refers mainly to the patient discussing his or her problems with a health professional. Licensed psychologists, psychiatrists, counselors, social workers, and ancillary mental health professionals all can provide this kind of therapy. In addition, dance therapy, music therapy, occupational therapy, recreational therapy, and art therapy can also all be used to help treat depression. After a hospitalized patient has progressed to the point of release from the hospital, he or she may enter a day-treatment program where therapy is provided on a daily basis, but the patient returns home each night. For many patients, day-treatment programs have successfully bridged the gap between the constant monitoring of in-patient status and a return to daily living activities.

Individual Psychological Therapy
The term *individual therapy* applies to a situation where a depressed patient speaks individually with a counselor, psychologist, psychiatrist, or some other type of therapist. The therapist will first try to make the person feel comfortable and at ease. This first step is very important in building a feeling of trust between therapist and patient. The ther-

apist will ask numerous questions to develop an understanding of the person's exact feelings and emotions. Once there is a good understanding of all aspects involved in the depression, the therapist and patient can then work together to develop a plan for counteracting the problem. The process of making changes in behavior and setting goals may take several months or years, and continued help may be necessary during this time. In some cases of severe depression, the person may have to be hospitalized for a time either in a special psychiatric unit in a general hospital or in a mental hospital. In either case the depressed person will receive individual and perhaps some other kinds of therapy daily.

If it is a child who is the depressed person, then the therapist will probably want to talk with the parents and may even hold meetings with the entire family. So-called family therapy can help each member of the family to understand why the person is depressed and what they, the family, can do to help.

Goals of Psychotherapy

The principal goals in psychotherapy are:

> Removal of symptoms and a relief of suffering
> Restoration of the level of everyday functioning that the patient possessed prior to the onset of the illness
> Promotion, if possible, of an understanding of the destructive patterns of behavior that sabotage functioning and interfere with the enjoyment of life
> In motivated patients, recognition of conflicting patterns of behavior and exploration of their meaning, origins, and consequences
> The providing of ways to deal with these patterns and their effects

If a precipitating event precedes the beginning of a depression by only a few weeks, it is easy to think of the event as being directly related to the depression. As the interval lengthens, however, the purported cause and effect relationship becomes more and more difficult to accept.

To get at the root of the depression, then, various types of psychotherapy are used. These include, among others, psychoanalysis, behavior therapy, hypnosis, group therapy, and psychodrama.

Psychoanalysis

Psychoanalysis focuses on the patient's unconscious thoughts and feelings as expressed in dreams, fantasies, and actions. According to psychoanalytic theory, the causes of many mental illnesses can lie buried deep in the unconscious. The patient meets with the psychiatrist or psychologist up to five times a week and talks about his or her childhood, dreams, or whatever else comes to mind. The therapist helps the patient understand his or her problems by uncovering unconscious conflicts. Resolution of these conflicts is viewed as being curative. Psychoanalysis may last for several years or longer.

Behavior Therapy

Behavior therapy uses the principles of conditioning and behavior modification to alleviate symptoms in a wide variety of mental disorders. Unlike classical psychotherapy, behavior therapy does not emphasize understanding the unconscious or release of emotional tensions. Behavior therapy is based on two underlying assumptions: (1) that the personality is a collection of learned habits, and (2) that disordered behavior is nothing more than the use of these habits in situations where they have no useful value. Treatment consists of eliminating the maladaptive habits by conditioning techniques and replacing these habits with more appropriate ones.

Psychodrama

Under the direction of a therapist, a group of patients are encouraged to act out their problems in drama form. They may play themselves or other people who are presently or were at one time actively involved in their lives. This type of acting out frequently helps a depressed person better understand his or her reaction to other people and environmental influences that may affect depressive behavior.

Group Therapy

Group therapy commonly involves a group of eight to twelve persons led by one or more therapists. Frequently, the depressed patient is helped by knowing that other people have similar problems and learns new ways of relating to other people. Some people talk about their problems better within the structure of a group setting led by a therapist than in individual therapy.

Hypnotherapy

The term *hypnotism* was first suggested by a Scottish surgeon named James Braid. It comes from the Greek word *hypnos*, meaning "sleep." Braid decided that the Greek word could be used to imply a sleeplike state, which is what hypnosis essentially is.

Toward the end of the last century, the interst in hypnotism for the treatment of a variety of illnesses and complaints was strong, especially in France. Jean Charcot, a prominent neurologist, used hypnosis to investigate various types of nervous conditions. It is interesting to note that Sigmund Freud, the father of modern psychiatry, studied under Charcot and brought the use of hypnosis back to Austria. After a period of using it in his treatment of mental illnesses, however, Freud became disenchanted with it and felt it was not a "real cure."

In recent years there has been a resurgence of interest in the psychological and medical use of hypnosis. State and national organizations are now certifying the proficiency of therapists in the use of "hypnotherapy." After a long and hard struggle, science may finally have found a place for the use of hypnosis in medicine.

WHAT IS HYPNOSIS?   Even today, scientists are still struggling to completely explain the phenomenon of hypnosis. They do know that the hypnotist has no special powers and that there is no magic involved. Hypnosis could be described as a special state of sleep, with unique properties. The hypnotized person appears to develop a heightened awareness of and sensitivity to the hypnotist's voice, words, and suggestions. The person's consciousness narrows much as it does during a dream. But different from sleep, the hypnotized person may be very active—walking about, talking, or writing. In 1955 the British Medical Association and in 1958 the American Medical Association adopted a tentative definition of hypnosis. They defined it as "a temporary condition of altered attention in the subject which may be induced by another person and in which a variety of phenomena may appear spontaneously or in response to verbal or other stimuli. These phenomena include alterations in consciousness and memory, increased susceptibility to suggestion, and the production in the subject of response and ideas unfamiliar to him in his usual state of mind. Further phenomena such as anesthesia, paralysis, and the rigidity of muscles, and phase of motor changes (sweating and blushing) can be produced as well as removed in hypnotic state."

During the induction of hypnosis the hypnotist relaxes the person by providing him or her with direct suggestions such as, "Your eyelids are getting heavy, your arms and legs are heavy and warm, and the muscles in your shoulders are very loose and limp." The person is instructed to breathe deeply, and suggestions are made for him or her to go into a deep sleep. Frequently, the hypnotist will instruct the person to look at a fixed point, such as a spot on the wall, a pencil, or even a spinning object on a string. Psychiatrists may use drugs to help a person relax and obtain a deeper state of hypnosis. Sodium-pentothal— "truth serum"—has been one of the most frequently used drugs, but with the new discovery of safer and more beneficial hypnotic drugs, sodium-pentothal has decreased in usage.

After a person has been induced into a hypnotic trance, suggestions are made to suit a wide variety of purposes. Under deep hypnosis, anesthesia, or the inability to feel pain, may be obtained, and surgical operations can be performed without the patient awakening from the hypnotic state. People in psychological therapy may be asked to recall events that they could not remember when awake. Forgetting painful experiences may also be suggested. Hypnosis today is also used to help people quit smoking, lose weight, overcome phobias, control the pain during childbirth, and so on.

The final stage of hypnosis is awakening from the trance. The hypnotist makes a suggestion that upon a certain signal, the subject will awaken, feeling refreshed and relaxed.

USE OF HYPNOSIS IN TREATING DEPRESSION   In treating depression, doctors may use hypnosis to give patients suggestions that will help them overcome depressive symptoms. If a depressed patient is a good hypnotic subject, then hypnosis, combined with other forms of therapy, may prove a very useful tool. Under hypnosis, patients can sometimes remember incidents or situations that they had completely forgotten that may be directly related to their feelings of depression. Hypnosis of severely depressed patients, however, has been found to be of little value.

The technique of suggesting to a depressed patient that he or she will feel better on awakening and will be able to behave differently—less self-destructively—in the future is called *post-hypnotic suggestion.* Post-hypnotic suggestions are most effective in patients who have been able to obtain a deep hypnotic trance.

PRECAUTIONS WITH HYPNOSIS   Hypnosis can be a very effective tool for helping some people overcome depression. Because hypnosis involves a person's physical and emotional functioning, however, it should only be performed by a professionally trained therapist. As with any therapy, careful attention should be directed toward selection of a qualified person. A qualified hypnotherapist will be certified by state and national organizations, attesting to his or her proficiency in the use of hypnosis. It is extremely unwise for anyone to ever allow himself or herself to be placed under hypnosis by anyone other than a qualified professional. A person seeking help through hypnosis should never hesitate to ask for a therapist's professional credentials.

ELECTROCONVULSIVE THERAPY

Electroconvulsive therapy (ECT) was introduced in 1935 by Laslow Joseph Maduna on the basis of two observations: patients would suddenly lose their symptoms when they had a spontaneous convulsion, and epilepsy and schizophrenia hardly ever occurred in the same patient. Ugo Cerletti used electroconvulsive therapy on psychotic patients in 1937 with his associate, Bini.

Maduna, Cerletti, Bini, and other early pioneers in the use of convulsive therapy soon discovered the treatment's usefulness, contraindications (when not to use), and complications. Before ECT was introduced, other investigators experimented with various convulsive agents of a drug nature.

The present use of ECT therapy is based upon its clear usefulness in a variety of illnesses, especially depression. Today, over 100,000 Americans a year receive electroconvulsive therapy treatments, usually for treatment of severe depression. Because of its potential for quick improvement, it is often used as an emergency measure when the depressed person is judged to be suicidal. Although antidepressive drugs are effective in removing symptoms for many depressed patients, usually a period of several weeks elapses before any improvement is seen, whereas sometimes only one or two ECT treatments are needed to lead to dramatic improvement. The exact reasons for the dramatic improvement are not fully understood, but there is recent evidence that biochemical changes in the brain produced by ECT may explain its effectiveness.

Throughout its history, ECT has been criticized as a form of treatment. The author Ernest Hemingway once stated that ECT treatments ruined his career as a writer because they extinguished his long-term memory of past experiences. During a recent session of the Washington State legislature, hearings were held on legislation to prohibit the use of ECT. During other hearings in various states, witnesses have testified about possible long-term memory loss or brain damage. Until the long-term effects of ECT are documented, the debate regarding its usefulness will continue.

Electroconvulsive therapy can be performed only by a physician and, in almost all cases, only by one who is a psychiatrist. ECT is usually performed in a psychiatric hospital or in a general hospital where other medical specialists may be present in the event complications should arise. The patient is given a sedative to relax, and a weak pulse of electricity is passed through the head to induce the brain into having a mini-seizure. Normally, the patient receiving ECT is scheduled for six to twelve treatments over a two-to-four week period, though as few as two treatments may be sufficient.

Changes During ECT

Scientists have noted that during ECT certain changes happen to the body. Hormonal changes are usually present along with an increase in weight. In women there may be menstrual cycle changes. Psychological changes usually consist of amnesia (memory loss) for the treatment period, and after several treatments some additional memory problems, which may last for some time. Some patients report a fear of the treatment which, before the first treatment, is probably due to the disquieting name of "shock treatment," but after several treatments seems to be a result of the unpleasant experience of waking up after the treatment and not knowing who one is for a while. Several other psychological and physical changes may occur during ECT. The exact reasons for these changes are still under investigation by scientists.

Complications During ECT

The most frequent complications in ECT prior to the administering of muscle relaxant drugs were broken bones. Fractures occurred when the muscles convulsed (tightened) during the treatment. Deaths were extremely rare, even before the introduction of anesthesia techniques in ECT.

Usually patients with a previous history of heart disease are monitored very carefully during this type of treatment, and the risk must be weighed against the possible benefits. ECT is usually avoided in patients suffering from brain tumors.

EXERCISE AND MEGAVITAMIN
THERAPY FOR DEPRESSION

The facts regarding physical benefits of regular exercise have been well documented. Lowering of body weight, strengthening of the heart and lungs, improved circulation, increased energy and stamina, more restful sleep, improved appearance, and a decrease in blood pressure have all been shown to result from a program of regular exercise.

Recent interest has turned toward the use of exercise as a method of preventing and treating depression. Researcher Robert S. Brown of the University of Virginia School of Medicine in Charlottesville examined the psychological effects of physical training in more than two thousand normal and depressed subjects over a period of five years. His research indicated that depressed patients showed significant improvement in anxiety levels after eight to ten weeks of noncompetitive jogging performed three times per week.

Brown noticed an even greater improvement when the patients were jogging five times per week. Brown feels that the act of jogging outdoors helps relieve stress through a change in the environment along with biochemical changes in the brain and bloodstream due to an increased production of norepinephrine brought about by the exercise. A deficiency in norepinephrine, it appears, can induce depression.

In a different approach, some physicians use massive doses of vitamins—especially niacin and vitamins B-6, B-12, C, and E—to help a person recover from depression. These doctors believe that the vitamins help restore the proper balance of chemicals in the brain. Such megavitamin treatment is usually used in combination with antidepressant drug therapy.

DRUG TREATMENT
FOR DEPRESSION

The story of antidepressant drugs begins with the fact that tuberculosis was a major chronic illness until about 1955. In 1952 preliminary reports suggested that a new drug, Isoniazid, was effective in treating tuberculosis; Isoniazid and similar antituberculosis drugs that came after were responsible for the emptying of hospital beds in the years that followed. One drug, Iproniazid, was introduced simultaneously with Isoniazid but was soon withdrawn as too toxic. Clinical reports on its use in tuberculosis treatment showed that there was considerable elevation of mood (less depression) in the patients receiving it. These reports were followed up, and the drug was reintroduced as an antidepressant agent in 1955 on the basis of promising early studies with depressed patients. Iproniazid is a monoamine oxidase inhibitor, and its discovery opened up a whole new class of compounds that could be used for treatment of severe depression. Monoamine oxidase was found to affect the levels of serotonin in the brain, which investigators believed influenced a person's ability to overcome depression.

Despite the early promise of monoamine oxidase, the number and severity of its side effects led to its ultimate demise. Iproniazid itself was removed from sale in 1961, after being implicated in at least fifty-four deaths. Furthermore, a recent study of the drug showed that in fifteen of thirty-one cases the monoamine oxidase drugs were no more effective than a placebo (fake drug). Therefore, because of their dangerous side effects and possible overall ineffectiveness, the use of this type of drug lost favor among physicians.

Imipramine left the testing laboratory when clinical tests showed that it reduced depression in a wide number of patients. Imipramine was the first of a series of drugs called tricyclics because of their chemical structure. Tricyclic compounds have been shown to reduce depression better than placebo treatment in more than 80 percent of scientific studies. They seem to work by increasing the available norepinephrine in the brain.

Methods for Taking Drugs

The two basic methods for induction of antidepressant drugs into the body are injection and oral administration. With a hypodermic syringe, chemicals can be delivered directly into the bloodstream or deposited in a muscle mass or under the upper layers of skin. With the intravenous (I.V.) injection, the drug starts in the bloodstream and does not have to be absorbed first, so that onset of action is faster than with any other form of administering drugs.

However, most drugs begin their entry into the body through the mouth. Taking antidepressant drugs orally is unquestionably the oldest and easiest route of administration. Still, it is not necessarily the most effective, since the drug in the digestive tract has to withstand the actions of the acid and digestive enzymes in the stomach and not be deactivated by food before it has been absorbed.

Using Antidepressant Drugs

Two hundred and fifty million prescriptions for antidepressant drugs are filled in the United States every year. Over $1 billion a year is spent on one major tranquilizer—Valium. In 1979 three million Americans took Valium as an aid to alleviating depression. Manic-depressives take a drug called lithium, which can help them lead more normal lives. For other depressions, the most widely used drugs are the tricyclics, sold under such brand names as Elavil and Tofranil.

Medication for depression may be prescribed only by medical doctors. Psychiatrists are medical doctors, but psychologists are not. Antidepressant drugs work well with certain types of depression but must always be carefully monitored by the physician. As with all medications, there may be side effects. Some of the more common side effects found with taking antidepressant medication are dizziness, weight gain, and, with elderly patients, a feeling of drunkenness or disorientation.

A depressed person taking antidepressant medication may not feel the results for several weeks. During this initial period, the medication may help the person to sleep better. When the drug has achieved its full effect, the patient will feel an increase in energy, headaches may disappear, and the tendency to cry or feel irritable will go away.

People taking medication must always be concerned about becoming addicted, or "hooked." However, antidepressant medications are generally not considered addictive. Antidepressant medications do not provide what is called a "high." A patient taking this type of medication is always told to contact his or her doctor immediately if any disturbing or uncomfortable side effects show up.

Lithium

One of the major contributions to American psychiatry of the past generation was the introduction of lithium carbonate, an ordinary mineral salt that can reverse the tendency toward bouts of bipolar depression; there is also evidence that it is effective in unipolar depression as well.

Lithium is an element and therefore cannot be patented, but its use was approved in 1970 by the Food and Drug Administration for the treatment of manic-depression. Interestingly, its medical use may date back to the fifth century B.C., in Greece, where the use of alkaline mineral spring water was suggested for the treatment of mania.

Lithium was used about a hundred years ago in the treatment of gout, but in the early part of the twentieth century its use was discontinued because of the side effects.

In the late 1940s, two medical uses of lithium and their results were reported almost simultaneously. Lithium chloride had been suggested and used with patients on low-sodium diets. Unfortunately, this use caused some fatalities, so no one was very interested in following up a report on lithium use that came out of Australia in 1949. The Australian report suggested strongly that mania and excitement were reduced when patients were given lithium carbonate.

Tryptophan

The newest discovery in biochemical treatment of depression is a substance named tryptophan, found in proteins such as meat, eggs, and milk. In tests at a West Suffolk hospital in England, tryptophan was used on nine depressed patients, and the antidepressant drug, Imipramine, was given to seven others. Both groups showed dramatic improvement over a four-week period, indicating that tryptophan was at least as effective as the prescription drug, and users did not risk having any side effects. Similar results were reported from tests in hospitals in Denmark, Finland, Norway, and Sweden. However, similar success has not been achieved in studies in the United States, and the FDA has not approved tryptophan for marketing as an antidepressant.

Asendin (Amoxapine)

Asendin is a new antidepressant drug developed by Lederle Laboratories. In contrast to the two to three weeks usually required to achieve antidepressant responses with Imipramine or other antidepressants, significant improvement often occurs within four to seven days with Asendin. This drug has been shown to relieve sleep disturbances in most patients, usually without affecting daytime alertness.

Sinequan (Doxepin HCL)

Sinequan has been found to be an effective antidepressant

with the convenience of a once-a-day nighttime dosage of the medication. In severe cases of depression a higher dosage of Sinequan may be given more than once daily. As with most of the new antidepressant medications, Sinequan helps to relieve the difficulty in falling and staying asleep and the early-morning awakening often associated with depression. This drug also works to relieve the anxiety that so often accompanies clinical depression. Drowsiness is the most commonly observed side effect. This drug is manufactured by Roerig, a division of Pfizer Pharmaceuticals.

Surmontil (Trimipramine Maleate)
As with most of the antidepressant medications, Surmontil works to relieve depression and anxiety partly, it seems, through improved sleep. In studies done by Ives Laboratory among depressed outpatients, a substantial majority had improved sleep patterns in the first week. This antidepressant achieves full effects after about two to four weeks of administration.

Additional Antidepressants
Most of the major pharmaceutical laboratories produce at least one antidepressant medication. Some additional antidepressant medications used by physicians are: Tofranil, Elavil, Limbitrol, Triavil, Adapin, and Ludiomil.

HOW DRUGS
HELP DEPRESSION

Antidepressant medications seem to give the depressed person a greater sense of control in dealing with the problems in his or her life. This does not mean that the person doesn't think about problems, but rather that when he or she does think about them, they do not cause an extreme sense of helplessness. The drugs do not cause happiness or elation, but they do help remove some of the feelings of helplessness and despair. This then allows the depressed person to deal with the problems and gradually eliminate or forget about them. The drugs also help the depressed person to feel less anxiety and sleep better.

Until 1958 the only two available means for helping to overcome depression were the use of psychotherapy and electroshock therapy. Now, with the constant improvement of antidepressant medication, many more patients are being helped who, in the past, would have continued to suffer.

Side Effects

As with any medication, there may be adverse (bad) side effects. Patients should always tell their doctor any side effects they are experiencing, so that the medication can be adjusted or discontinued.

Some of the adverse side effects of antidepressant medication are:

Excessive excitement
Dry mouth
Constipation
Dizziness
Rapid heartbeat
Blurred vision
Difficulty in urinating
Weight gain
Skin rashes

THE BODY'S BUILT-IN ANTIDEPRESSANTS

During a recent seminar at the College of William and Mary in Williamsburg, Virginia, sponsored by the National Institute of Mental Health, some of the world's leading physicians, neurologists, and neuroendocrinologists discussed some rather startling findings concerning the role of body functions when a person is depressed. The results were the product of years of investigation by researchers from all over the world. New information was reported on the action of neurotransmitter substances (messengers) in the brain and their relationship to depression. These discoveries represent the first breakthroughs in the search for the chemical causes of depression.

Scientists have discovered two substances which everyone manufactures within his or her own body and which can actually fight depression and monitor stress. They are norepinephrine and serotonin. Both were mentioned earlier in this book. In simple terms, the adrenal glands, activated by environmental stress or exercise, determine the amount of epinephrine in the human body. Epinephrine serves as an activator to norepinephrine and serotonin. These chemicals are manufactured by the brain to aid in the sending of nerve impulses throughout the body. Studies have shown that people who lack norepinephrine are more likely to be tired, listless, and depressed. In addition, it is the serotonin mechanism that controls the flow of oxygen.

Researchers around the world are now concentrating on the discovery that certain foods and exercise actually stimulate the production of these antidepressant chemicals created within the body.

CHAPTER SIX

HELPING THE DEPRESSED PERSON

Although depression may be a very serious problem, family and friends can do much to help. Treating the depressed person as normally as possible and keeping the individual busy and active can be useful. Some depressed people become apathetic and inactive, which leads to more depression and more inactivity. Helping a depressed person with gentle suggestions regarding activities may be very helpful.

Depression typically involves strong feelings of guilt, and it is important that family and friends do not make the depression worse by blaming the person for his or her depression. It is tempting to become impatient with a depressed person and to tell him or her to "snap out of it" or to say that depression is a sign of weakness. Most depressed people need understanding and help, not criticism.

When a depressed person does not respond to the help provided by friends and family, then professional help should be sought.

Even when the depression appears mild, the possibility of suicide should not be excluded. A mental health professional should be consulted whenever a clinical depressive disorder is suspected. The earlier a depressed person receives help, the sooner the symptoms are alleviated and the quicker the recovery.

People no longer have to suffer from the devastating symptoms of depression, for today it is the most treatable of all illnesses. With modern treatment methods and help from family and friends, individuals can return to full and productive lives.

SUGGESTIONS FOR
HELPING TO OVERCOME
DEPRESSION

The following suggestions for overcoming a mild depression you yourself may be experiencing have been compiled from information provided by psychiatrists, psychologists, counselors, and other mental health professionals:

1. Create order in your life. Do the things you've always done. Maintain regular habits. Then reflect on these small accomplishments; they will make you feel more worthy and competent.

2. Keep up appearances. Letting yourself and your living quarters fall apart only strengthens the idea that there is nothing to look "good" for.

3. Don't give up a project; try to make things in your life matter.

4. Don't suppress anger. Resigning yourself to mistreatment makes you believe that you deserve it, and that you'll always get it. There is a deadly

calm in depression. Take every opportunity to feel strongly and act on your feelings.

5. Study and learn something new each day. It gives you the sense that there is something new, and better, in the future.

6. Stop talking about your problems for a specific period. Talk can perpetuate them and make you feel that you have nothing else to offer.

7. Take note of the good moments in your life, especially the unexpected ones. Open yourself to potentially pleasurable events.

8. Spend time with people who are energetic and hopeful.

MAKING A REFERRAL FOR THERAPY

Trying to convince a depressed person of the need to seek professional therapy is probably one of the most difficult tasks facing a family member or friend of a depressed person. Superstitions and misinformation abound in regard to seeking professional help. Some common statements that people may make when suggestions of referral are made are, "I'm not going to see a shrink; everyone will think I'm crazy!" "If they put me in a mental hospital I'll never get out!" "If my boss finds out I'll be fired." "I can work it out myself, without anybody's help." "No one can help me, it's past that point."

Helping someone overcome the fear of seeking professional help can be very difficult. Providing the depressed person with accurate, easy-to-understand, pertinent information regarding depression and its treatment may help overcome some of the initial fears. Many times the depressed person will not seek help unless information is provided by a friend or loved one. State mental health agencies, hospitals, therapists, and the government all provide publications designed specifically to help the depressed person overcome the initial hurdle in seeking help.

GLOSSARY

Antidepressant drugs—psychoactive drugs used to treat severe depression, including Doxepin (Sinquan), Imipramine, and Amitriptyline (Elavil).

Anxiety—a sense of fear, unease, or apprehension that appears to have no defined cause.

Behavioral therapy—psychoanalytic therapy that involves changing behavior, or habits, without necessarily finding out the root causes of that behavior.

Bipolar depression—see *Manic-depressive psychosis.*

Clinical depression—depression that is enduring and appears to have no direct cause; depression that does or should come to the attention of a mental health professional. Clinical depression can range from mild to moderate to severe.

Counseling—a helping profession in which assistance is offered in terms of suggestions, alternatives, or aid in finding suitable solutions to problems.

Depressive disorder—a neurosis or psychosis in which the principal feature is a strong feeling of sadness, apathy, or helplessness that is persistent and interferes with normal functioning. Also called clinical depression, a depressive neurosis is not as severe as a depressive psychosis.

ECT—electroconvulsive therapy, in which an electric current is used to stimulate the central nervous system through electrodes attached to the head of a severely disturbed patient. It produces a convulsive seizure that is controlled with medication.

Electroconvulsive therapy—see *ECT*, above.

Family therapy—a form of therapy that focuses on the entire family in order to find solutions to problems and improve relationships among family members. Primarily used to help one family member who is experiencing difficulties.

Genetic trait—a hereditary characteristic passed from parent to child through the genes.

Group therapy—a group form of psychotherapy that brings together several persons with the same or related problems and deals with them through simultaneous therapy with one or several therapists.

Hypnosis—a state of mind that resembles sleep but has been induced by a hypnotist; the subject under hypnosis is very susceptible to suggestions made by the hypnotist. Hypnotism is sometimes used in psychoanalytic therapies for recalling forgotten or repressed memories from the unconscious.

Lithium—a drug used to control unipolar depressive illness plus the wide mood swings of a person who suffers from a manic-depressive disorder.

Major tranquilizers—A group of psychoactive drugs that are used to reduce anxiety. They are used most commonly in the treatment of severe disorders such as psychoses.

Mania—a neurotic or psychotic state showing excessive elation or hyperactivity. It can alternate with depression in some patients.

Manic-depressive psychosis—a disorder characterized by wide variations in mood, from euphoria to severe depression. Today usually called bipolar depression.

Melancholia—extreme or overwhelming sadness that goes on and on. This clinical condition is also characterized by an inability to feel pleasure.

Mental illness—any disorder of behavior, mood, thinking, or feeling that prevents a person from functioning normally.

Minor tranquilizers—drugs used for the treatment of mild, or neurotic, disorders that produce anxiety or stress.

Neurosis—a disorder characterized by identifiable symptoms that causes anxiety, mood change, or other distress that interferes with normal functioning of the person. The symptoms are not of organic origin, endure over time, and are not severely different from normal.

Norepinephrine—a brain chemical thought to play a part in severe depression.

Postpartum depression—depression following childbirth; very common and usually goes away by itself, without need of professional treatment.

Psychiatrist—a medical doctor who specializes in the treatment of mental disorders.

Psychoanalyst—a psychiatrist, psychologist, or other psychotherapist who has received certification from a recognized psychoanalytic institute and who uses the method of psychoanalysis—conversation—in the treatment of mental disorders.

Psychodrama—the acting out, or role-playing, of situations, in order to better understand one's feelings and thoughts. Psychodrama is used in many forms of psychoanalytic therapies for uncovering unconscious thoughts and desires.

Psychologist—a person who specializes in the study and treatment of human behavior. Usually holds a Ph.D. degree; may specialize in one of several specialty areas in psychology such as clinical, counseling, industrial, or social.

Psychosis—a severe mental disorder that interferes with or prevents entirely normal day-to-day functioning.

Psychosomatic diseases—diseases brought on by emotional states. Psychosomatic diseases are very real and often cause great harm to the body.

Psychotherapist—a person who has had professional training in the treatment of mental or personality disorders and who uses psychological methods.

Psychotherapy—any of a wide variety of treatment methods used by psychotherapists to help a patient solve behavioral problems. The principal means of therapy is talk between the patient and the therapist.

Serotonin—a body chemical thought to be involved in depression.

Stress—a reaction of the body and/or personality to events in the environment. When positive, provides motivation for action. When negative, can cause physical symptoms and/or psychological distress.

Unipolar depression—depression only; distinguished from bipolar depressive illness, which typically involves episodes of mania alternating with depression.

Valium—perhaps the most widely used minor tranquilizer. Valium is not usually prescribed in the treatment of severe depression.

FOR
FURTHER
INFORMATION
OR
PROFESSIONAL
HELP

American Association of Suicidology
c/o Merck, Sharp, and Dohme
Division of Merck and Company, Inc.
West Point, PA 19468

American Academy of Child Psychiatry
1424 16th Street N.W.
Suite 201A
Washington, DC 20036

American Academy of Clinical Psychiatrists
Vine Street Clinic
Stuart Building
610 East Vine Street
Springfield, IL 62703

American Academy of Psychotherapists
6363 Roswell Road
Atlanta, GA 30328

American Association for Geriatric Psychiatry
230 North Michigan Avenue
Suite 2400
Chicago, IL 60601

American Association for Social Psychiatry
201 South Livingston Avenue
Livingston, NJ 07039

American Association of Psychiatric Services for Children
1725 K Street N.W.
Washington, DC 20006

American Family Therapy Association
15 Bond Street
Great Neck, NY 11021

American Mental Health Foundation
2 East 86th Street
New York, NY 10028

American Psychiatric Association
1700 18th Street N.W.
Washington, DC 20009

American Psychoanalytic Association
1 East 57th Street
New York, NY 10022

American Psychological Association
1200 17th Street N.W.
Washington, DC 20036

American Psychotherapy Association
P.O. Box 2436
West Palm Beach, FL 33402

Association for Advancement of Behavior Therapy
420 Lexington Avenue
New York, NY 10017

Association for Research in Nervous and Mental Disease
Mount Sinai School of Medicine
100th Street at Fifth Avenue
New York, NY 10029

Depression Evaluation Service
722 West 168th Street
New York, NY 10032

Family Service Association of America
44 East 23rd Street
New York, NY 10010

Foundation for Depression and Manic Depression
7 East 67th Street
New York, NY 10021

Institute on Hospital and Community Psychiatry
1700 18th Street N.W.
Washington, DC 20009

Mental Health Association
1800 North Kent Street
Rosslyn, VA 22209

Mental Health Materials Center
419 Park Avenue South
New York, NY 10016

Mental Health Research Foundation
72 Burroughs Place
Bloomfield, NY 07003

National Association for Mental Health
250 West 57th Street
Room 1425
New York, NY 10019

National Association of Private Psychiatric Hospitals
1701 K Street N.W.
Suite 1205
Washington, DC 20006

National Council of Community Mental Health Centers
2233 Wisconsin Avenue N.W.
Suite 322
Washington, DC 20007

National Institute of Mental Health
5600 Fishers Lane
Rockville, MD 20857

U.S. Department of Health and Human Services
Alcohol, Drug Abuse, and Mental Health Administration
5600 Fishers Lane
Rockville, MD 20857

PAMPHLETS

SOURCE	PAMPHLET TITLE
Blue Cross Association 840 N. Lake Shore Dr. Chicago, IL 60611	*Stress*, 1974, 96 pp.
Mental Health Association 1800 N. Kent St. Arlington, VA 22209	*Facts About Mental Illness* *How to Deal with Mental* *Problems*

*How to Deal with Your
    Tensions
Mental Illness Can Be
    Prevented
New Directions for
    Community Mental Health
Some Things You Should
    Know About Mental Illness*

National Clearinghouse for
Mental Health Information
5600 Fishers Lane
Rockville, MD 20857

*Causes, Detection, and
    Treatment of Childhood
    Depression,* NIH Pubn.
    no. (ADM) 78-612
*Citizens' Guide to
    Community Mental Health
    Centers, Amendments of
    1975, 1977,* NIH Pubn.
    no. (ADM) 77-397
*Consumer's Guide to Mental
    Health Services,* 1975,
    NIH Pubn. no. (ADM) 75-
    214
*It's Good to Know About
    Mental Health,* 1977, NIH
    Pubn. no. (ADM) 77-67
*Learning About Depressive
    Illnesses,* 1977, NIH Pubn.
    no. (ADM) 77-288
*Lithium in the Treatment of
    Mood Disorders,* 1977,
    NIH Pubn. no. (ADM)
    77-73
*Mental Health Matters:
    Depression,* 1978, NIH
    Pubn. no. (ADM) 78-601

Plain Talk About Stress,
1978, NIH Pubn. no.
(ADM) 78-502

Public Affairs Committee,
Inc.
381 Park Avenue
New York, NY 10016

*Dealing with the Crisis of
Suicide*, No. 406A
*Depression: Causes and
Treatment*, No. 488
*Helping Children Face
Crises*, No. 541
How to Cope with Crises,
No. 464
*Mental Health is a Family
Affair*, No. 155
Understanding Stress, No.
538

BIBLIOGRAPHY

Abramson, L. Y.; Seligman, M. E. P.; and Teasdale, J. D. "Learned Helplessness in Humans: Critique and Reformulation." *Journal of Abnormal Psychology* 87: 49–74.

American Psychiatric Association. "The Current Status of Lithium Therapy: Report of the APA Task Force." *American Journal of Psychiatry* 132: 997–1001.

———.*Diagnostic and Statistical Manual of Mental Disorders*. 3rd ed., 1980.

Beck, A. T. *Depression: Clinical, Experimental, and Theoretical Aspects*. New York: Hoebner, 1967.

Bry, Adelaide. *Getting Better*. New York: Rawson, Wade, 1979.

Cammer, Leonard. *Up from Depression*. New York: Simon and Schuster, 1969.

Cronbach, L. J. *Essentials of Psychological Testing*. 2nd ed. New York: Harper & Row, 1970.

Friedberg, John. *Shock Treatment Is Not Good for Your Brain*. San Francisco: Glide Publications, 1976.

Geron, M. E., and Cadoret, R. J. "Genetic Aspects of Manic-depressive Disease in Family Practice." *Journal of Family Practice* 4: 453–456.

Herrink, Richie. *The Psychotherapy Handbook.* New York: Meridian, 1980.

Kiev, Ari. *Courage to Live.* New York: T. Y. Crowell, 1979.

Lewinsohn, Peter M., et al. *Control Your Depression* (Self-Management Series). Englewood Cliffs, NJ: Prentice-Hall, 1979.

Murphy, D. L. "Neuropharmacology and Depression," *Drug Treatment of Mental Disorders*, edited by L. L. Simpson. New York: Raven Press, 1976.

Park, Clara Clairborne, with Leon N. Shapiro. *You Are Not Alone: Understanding and Dealing with Mental Illness. A Guide for Patients, Families, Doctors, and Other Professionals.* Boston: Little Brown, 1979.

Scarf, Maggie. *Unfinished Business: A Study of Depression in Women.* New York: Ballantine Books, 1981.

Shaffer, D. "Suicide In Childhood and Early Adolescence." *Journal of Child Psychology and Psychiatry* 15: 275–291.

INDEX

ABOUT
THE AUTHOR

NEAL H. OLSHAN
is a psychologist with a private practice
and is also director of the
Southwest Pain Treatment Center
in Scottsdale, Arizona.

He is the coauthor of one previous book
for Franklin Watts, entitled
Fears and Phobias: Fighting Back (1980).

He has also written several books for adults,
including one on chronic pain.